KT-416-082

SUMMONS TO FAITH AND RENEWAL

*Pastoral Renewal Books are published by
Servant Books in cooperation with The Center
for Pastoral Renewal.*

Summons to Faith and Renewal

Christian Renewal in a Post-Christian World

Edited by
Peter Williamson and Kevin Perrotta

 A *Pastoral Renewal* Book

SERVANT BOOKS
Ann Arbor, Michigan

Copyright © 1983 by The Center for Pastoral Renewal

Cover and book design by John B. Leidy

Available from Servant Books, Box 8617, Ann Arbor,
Michigan 48107

83 84 85 10 9 8 7 6 5 4 3 2 1

ISBN 0-89283-135-9
Printed in the United States of America

Library of Congress Cataloging in Publication Data
Main entry under title:

Summons to faith and renewal.

    Contents: Self, Jesus, and God / James Hitchcock —
Faith, life, and the spirit of the age / Harold O.J.
Brown — The attack on God's word, and the response /
Ralph C. Martin — [etc.]
    1. Christianity—20th century—Congresses.
2. Christian union—Congresses. 3. Church renewal—
Congresses. I. Williamson, Peter, 1951-
II. Perrotta, Kevin.
BR121.2.S79 1983   262′.0017   83-12842
ISBN 0-89283-135-9 (pbk.)

Contents

Contributors

Harold O.J. Brown is professor of theology, Trinity Evangelical Divinity School, Deerfield, Illinois, and a founder of the Christian Action Council. His books include *Christianity and the Class Struggle* and *Death before Birth*.

Stephen B. Clark is the overall coordinator of The Word of God, an interdenominational Christian community in the Ann Arbor, Michigan, area. His books include *Building Christian Communities* and *Man and Woman in Christ*.

James Hitchcock is professor of history, St. Louis University, and a founder and past president of the Fellowship of Catholic Scholars. His books include *The Loss of the Sacred* and *Catholicism and Modernity*.

Mark Kinzer is senior elder of the Free Church Fellowship of The Word of God, Ann Arbor, Michigan. He is the author of *The Self-Image of a Christian* and *Taming the Tongue*.

Ralph C. Martin is the director of Renewal Ministries. His books include *Hungry for God* and *A Crisis of Truth*.

James I. Packer is professor of historical and systematic theology, Regent College, Vancouver, Canada. His books include *Knowing God* and *Beyond the Battle for the Bible*.

Peter S. Williamson is director of the Center for Pastoral Renewal, the editor of *Pastoral Renewal* journal, and the author of *How to Become the Person You Were Meant to Be*. He was the chairman of the conference from which the present book comes.

Preface

THE ESSAYS IN THIS BOOK are the product of an unusual meeting of Protestant, Catholic, and Orthodox leaders who share some common concerns for the welfare of the Christian people at the close of the twentieth century. The conference was held in Ann Arbor, Michigan, in October 1982, and was convened at the initiative of the Center for Pastoral Renewal, an organization that has developed from the work of *Pastoral Renewal,* a publication that seeks to foster spiritual and pastoral renewal within the churches.

The 130 or so leaders who gathered in Ann Arbor came with a concern for the confrontation between Christianity and modernity. It was their common desire to see preserved intact the fundamental teaching about faith and morals that Christians share, in the face of the powerful secular ideologies and mindset the churches confront today. The conferees also gathered with the desire to preserve—and to some degree recover—a way of life distinct from surrounding society by its faithfulness to the teaching of Christ. Those who convened the conference and those who attended it are convinced that these objectives cannot be attained either by simply fighting for orthodoxy or by a return to the church life of an earlier era. What is needed is a comprehensive and faithful presentation and living out of Christianity that is effective in the unique conditions of modern society. Also needed is a widespread turning to the Lord in faith and repentance, asking that in his mercy he intervene and renew his people.

This book and the conference that produced it are the second stage in a movement of Christians of different traditions coming together to address these issues. In October 1980 the first conference was held, and the results were published under the title *Christianity Confronts Modernity* (Williamson and Perrotta, eds., Servant Publications, 1981). That volume focused on various arenas of confrontation between Christianity and modernity. It opened with a pastoral analysis of some of the unique social characteristics of the modern age by Mark Kinzer, followed by examinations of Christians' confrontation with modernity in their political thinking (Dale Vree), in their assumptions in church work (James Hitchcock), in the fields of psychology and counseling (Paul Vitz), and in the study of scripture (Stephen B. Clark). The conference concluded with Donald Bloesch's call for an alliance of Christians of different traditions (evangelical Protestants and Roman Catholics) around the kinds of theological and pastoral issues which the conference addressed.

The present volume, based on the second conference, builds on the conclusions of the first. It amplifies the first book's analysis of the pressures that modern life brings to bear on Christian thought and behavior, and it summons all who will listen to respond. The summons involves, first of all, faithfulness to God and to his word, and secondly, earnestly devoting ourselves to seeking the renewal of the churches through prayer and through our pastoral and apostolic labors.

The first three essays address distortions present in some contemporary theological thought. James Hitchcock, a Roman Catholic, examines currents of thought that depart from historic Christianity, particularly as they are found in the teaching of Roman Catholics and mainline Protestants. Harold O.J. Brown extends this analysis to an examination of tendencies among evangelical Protestants. Ralph Martin, citing examples from each of these theological traditions, uncovers the root of these errors: a rejection of the authority of God's word.

My own essay completes the first half of the book by examining trends among the Christian people which suggest that, besides the tendency to accommodate Christian teaching to secular patterns of thought, there is an equally serious tendency for Christians' way of life to be conformed to the surrounding non-Christian society.

In the second half of the book, Stephen Clark sets forth the foundations of the ecumenism that characterizes the emerging movement of Christians in response to these developments. This is not an ecumenism of doctrinal compromise, with a unity shaped by a common secular agenda; nor is it the legitimate ecumenism of dialogue, in which doctrinal differences are explored by theologians from different traditions for the sake of greater mutual understanding. It is, instead, a cooperative ecumenism, based on a concern for the common problems and needs that beset Christians in the modern situation, and on the theological fact of our unique brotherhood and sisterhood in Christ.

James Packer and Mark Kinzer summon us to seek the renewal of the church. James Packer defines genuine renewal theologically as the infusion of spiritual life in Christian experience by the Holy Spirit. He goes on to describe its features and concludes by outlining steps for seeking such a renewal. Mark Kinzer follows by describing biblical norms for Christian living that ought to shape pastoral goals, and by identifying some essential practical tools for pastoring Christians in the modern world.

It is possible that some readers who wholeheartedly share the concerns this volume addresses will not be fully satisfied with these essays, desiring analyses or proposals which go further and are more specific. To some degree their desires may be met by the volume which precedes this one (described above) or by some of the workshops held at the conference, all of which were taped and some of which we expect will be published later in some form. Those who are interested in audio tapes of the workshops may write the Center for Pastoral Renewal for more information. In a few cases printed copies of the workshops are also available.*

But it is quite possible that neither of these resources will satisfy the ardent, and that the incompleteness they sense is a necessary stage inherent in the nature of the cooperation we are attempting. It would be a mistake to underestimate the difficulty of drawing together Christians from so broad a spectrum of theological persuasions in such a way that a common understanding of the issues and solutions develops. This is a task that calls for careful building and for patience. If the blueprint is sound, and if the Lord builds the house, we will not regret time spent in careful measurements as the foundations are laid.

Surely the most exciting aspect of the conference was not the novelty of what was said but the diversity of church traditions represented, and the diversity of kinds of Christian leaders— scholars, lay and ordained pastoral leaders, authors and journalists—participating in the common effort. This second conference was an advance on the first by virtue of the inclusion of Orthodox leaders along with the Protestants and Roman Catholics already involved. Their number was small, but it included such prominent leaders as theologian Stanley Harakas,

---

*The workshops were:

Paul C. Vitz, "Christian Perspectives on Moral Education"

Howard A. Snyder, "Characteristics of a Healthy Church"

George A. Kelly and Charles W. Keysor, "The Churches Confront Modernity: The Roman Catholic Church and the United Methodist Church"

Bert Ghezzi, "Designing a Modern Didache"

Charles E. Hummel and Ralph C. Martin, "The Charismatic Renewal: Strengths, Weaknesses, and Lessons: A Protestant View and a Catholic View"

Mark S. Kinzer and Germain Grisez, "Christianity and the Decline of Western Civilization: A Sociological View and Notes Towards an Updating of *The City of God*"

James Hitchcock, "Institutional Responses to the Crisis of Truth: A Case Study of Theology and Political Power"

Humberto Belli, "Central America, 1967-1982"

scripture scholar Theodore Stylianopoulos, and the chancellor of the western diocese of the Orthodox Church of America, Thaddeus Wojcik. Also present at the conference were scholars and educators such as Hudson T. Armerding, Karl Heintz, Paul Vitz, Howard Snyder, Ronald Lawler, George Kelly, Charles Keysor, and Richard Lovelace; church leaders such as Catholic Bishop Kenneth Povish, Richard Malone (of the Catholic Bishops' Conference), and Evangelical Orthodox Bishop Frederick Rogers; leaders of renewal communities or organizations such as Philip Merdinger of the People of Hope, psychiatrist Kevin Murrell, and Inter-Varsity leader Keith Hunt; authors such as Ronda Chervin and Gladys Hunt; publishers such as Harold and Luci Shaw; and journalists such as Dean Merrill of *Leadership* and Greg Erlandson of *The National Catholic Register*.

Another unique feature of the conference was that it brought together two streams which have heretofore run in fairly different channels. From among both Catholics and Protestants the conference drew together people whose primary interests have been evangelism, renewal, and church growth, with people who have been mainly concerned with the battle for faithfulness to historic Christian teaching within their respective churches. One of the themes of the conference was that these two concerns are related. It is neither desirable nor possible to maintain doctrine that is faithful to God's word without spiritual vitality and a healthy church life. And it is equally impossible to preach the gospel and bring spiritual renewal to large numbers of people when the doctrinal foundations are in disarray; to do so is to gather the harvest in baskets full of holes. Today the church is summoned by its Lord to both faithfulness and renewal.

At the conclusion of the conference the Center for Pastoral Renewal established the Alliance for Faith and Renewal, an association to enable those who participated in the conferences, and other interested Christians, to pursue the concerns of the conferences. Readers of this volume who are interested in learning more about the Alliance should write the Center for

Pastoral Renewal, Box 8617, Ann Arbor, Michigan 48107. A statement of purpose for the Alliance is published following this preface.

The essays published here are essentially the same as they were when presented at the conference, except for minor changes by their authors. Chapter Four, "The Loss of a Christian Way of Life," was presented at the conference in a shorter form as part of my introductory remarks at the meeting. Also, the introduction to this book, which offers a historical perspective on the issues confronting Christians which the conference participants gathered to address, has been written especially for this volume by Kevin Perrotta, the conference's program coordinator.

The agendas for theology, ethics, and psychology included at the end of the book represent the proposals of the individuals under whose names they appear, together with their summaries of the perspectives of others who participated in workshops on these themes. Finally, at the front of the book there is the statement of purpose of the Alliance for Faith and Renewal, the organization initiated at the conference to carry on the task of addressing these issues.

We who organized the conference and who edited this volume count it a unique privilege to participate in this effort of Christians from diverse backgrounds to take a common concern for the condition of the whole Christian people and the challenges that confront them today. We hope you will consider joining us in this work. Those who are interested in doing so may use the membership form that appears at the end of the book.

Peter S. Williamson

Alliance for Faith and Renewal:
A Statement of Purpose

WE ARE CHRISTIANS who want to work together for the cause of Christ. We want to see the message and teaching of Christ presented clearly in the churches and to the world, and to see individual Christians and the Christian churches renewed in a living relationship with God.

Confident though we are in Christ's lordship, we see that the increasingly de-Christianized societies of the West present a difficult environment for Christian life and mission. Many of the structures of the modern world tend to undermine Christians' ability to maintain their distinctiveness from the secularist cultures they live in. We believe that Christians must strengthen their relationships with one another in order to better meet these challenges. We recognize the necessity of Christians living by the teaching of Christ—being a holy nation, a people set apart with a distinct way of life.

We also observe a widespread secularization of Christian teaching and ministry. In light of this, we see the need for Christians of all confessional traditions to join together to reassert the fundamental elements of the Christian faith we hold in common.

We believe that the Christian people must unite in loyalty to the authority of God's word. Today faith in God's revelation, and obedience to it, is being attacked, both directly and indirectly, outside and inside the churches. This is an assault that all Christians must resist.

As a group of Protestants, Catholics, and Orthodox, we recognize one another as brothers and sisters in Christ, separated by important differences of belief and church order but united in our desire to obey one Lord. Many of the challenges we face in our own churches are common challenges that confront all Christians today. Therefore we want to work together for a better understanding of these challenges, fostering communication, and supporting one another in our respective roles of service to the Christian people.

Desiring to see a renewal of God's life in his people, we know that renewal must begin in our individual lives with repentance from sin, wholehearted commitment to Christ, and reliance on the power of the Holy Spirit. Moreover, we pray for God to intervene in all his people's lives, pardoning us, strengthening us, and extending his kingdom through us.

It is our intention to put our commitment to Christ and his cause in the world above everything else. We want to work together in practical ways to strengthen one another as Christians, to defend Christian teaching, and to bring the world to Christ.

Christianity Confronts Modernity

THIS BOOK ISSUES A SUMMONS to all Christians to reaffirm their adherence to the central tenets of the Christian faith and to join together in the work of spiritual and pastoral renewal. The authors speak with a sense of urgency. Today unusual opportunities and difficulties confront those who have identified themselves with the cause of Christ in the world. In this introduction I will attempt to sketch some of what makes the modern situation of Christianity unique—the configuration of social, intellectual, and spiritual forces that pose a different challenge to the churches today than Christianity faced in its first eighteen hundred years. In what follows I will not speak directly about the particular chapters of this book but about the context in which the summons as a whole has developed.

The Significance of Social Change

A serious weakness in the churches today is the failure to grasp the ways in which many problems facing Christianity are rooted in the peculiar social conditions of the modern world. There is no lack of awareness that problems exist; any pastor can tell you about the obstacles to Christian living that people deal with. And there is a general awareness that our world is quite different from that of our ancestors. But there has been little careful thinking about the relationship between the problems of

1

the churches and the social characteristics of modernity.

For example, Catholics in the United States are quite concerned about the sharp drop since 1965 in the number of men seeking to become priests. Studies reveal priests' own questioning of their role and the diminishing desire of Catholic parents to see their sons become priests. These factors, in turn, are rooted in social changes: alterations in the life of the American Catholic community, such as suburbanization, rising education, and affluence, have contributed to the crisis in how priests perceive their role of leadership; Catholics' changing position in American society—absorption into the mainstream—has altered the aspirations that parents cherish for their sons. Too little effort has been invested in tracing causes such as these and in finding fundamental solutions to them. Instead, attempts to remedy the decline in seminary enrollment have focused on organizational solutions, such as recruitment techniques.

To give another example, there is the response of conservative Protestants to the disintegration of the family. Joseph Bayly, a respected evangelical commentator, wrote in early 1983: "We are all familiar with the increasing trend toward divorce and the single-parent home in American society. Evangelical Christians are experiencing the same trend. . . . From a long-range viewpoint, this breakdown of Christian marriage and family is the most ominous cloud on the horizon."[1] Yet where are the studies which would tell us what it is about evangelical church life which, in confrontation with contemporary secularist society, is now giving way after so many years of a strongly countercultural stance?

Moreover, we need not only an investigation of the changes within various groupings of Christians that are causing them increasingly to abandon their distinctive attitudes and behavior; it is also necessary to ask what it is about the structures of *everyone's* lives in modern society that gives such powerful impetus to non-Christian attitudes and behavior. That is to say, the question is not only why Christians are tending to look more like everyone else, but also why everyone else is looking the way they are. What is it about the arrangements of family life, child rearing, schooling, work, leisure, etc., that reinforces the reigning secular values and customs?

That a relationship does exist between the structures of modern life and the advance of de-Christianization is strongly suggested by a consideration of the steady increase in family instability and sexual promiscuity which has accompanied the continuing technological revolution of the last two centuries. In fact, the disintegration of the family and the entire sexual revolution of which it is a part are key realities for understanding both the conditions of Christian life today and the social processes of modernization. To examine this congeries of problems is to hold several threads in hand—the high incidence of divorce, the acceptance of sexual activity outside marriage, the decreasing ability of parents to mold their children's values, and so on. We can follow some of these threads backwards in time with hard data; other threads we can trace less precisely.

The threads of divorce and premarital sexual activity we can trace back through periods when these practices were successively less frequent. We can follow the rates of incidence through the early 1970s and the late 1960s, when a sudden upsurge occurred throughout North America and Western Europe. We can go back through the early 20th and the 19th centuries, when there were gradually rising levels of divorce and premarital sexual activity in the West. It is not until we retrace the rates across the massive divide of modernization, back to the largely rural world of preindustrial Europe, that we find a period when the great mass of people in all Western societies were faithful to Christian teaching about the permanence of marriage and the restriction of sexual activity to marriage. We have come to our present problems with divorce and premarital sexual activity through a long historical process. What we are experiencing in Western societies is only the latest stage of a breakdown in husband-wife relationships and in sexual morality which got underway in the second half of the 18th century, about the time the first spinning jennies and power looms were being set up in Lancashire. Many Christians have been and are being carried along in these long-term trends.

Another aspect of family disintegration—the diminution of parental influence over children—is a thread less easily traced with figures (although rising rates of teenage illegitimacy are an indication). There does seem to have been a measurable decline in the late 1960s throughout the West in older children's inclination to live under their parents' authority and adopt their values—an increase not in adolescent hostility to parents but in indifference to their views. While the picture is not entirely clear for the early 20th and the 19th centuries, it is certain that a very different pattern prevailed in the West before the onset of modernization. In traditional society, older children seem to have been somewhat less influenced directly by their parents than we might suppose, but they were heavily influenced by the village and local community, sometimes especially by one component of that community—the peer group of young adults. The crucial difference between then and now is that formerly the extraparental influences tended to channel young people into traditional ways of life, while today the influences outside the home often attract young people to nontraditional ways—which means values and behavior distant from Christianity. Again, a serious pastoral problem—parents' difficulty passing on their values and way of life to their children—is entwined with processes of change that arose more than two centuries ago. This has become an especially acute problem for Christians in recent years.

The phenomenon repeats itself over and over: serious issues in respect to the integrity of Christian life and thought in our day turn out to be bound up with social forces that took shape with the coming of the modern world. If we ask questions such as why people's, including Christians', beliefs and behavior are susceptible to such rapid and unpredictable change in modern society, or why there are so many Christians in the United States yet so little Christian social impact, or many other questions, we are driven again and again to consider the fundamental changes that have made our world so different from the world in any previous age.

Unfortunately, many of these changes have not seemed very interesting to many thinkers. Mundane changes in how the great masses of ordinary people live lack the dramatic qualities of the doings of the rich and the powerful that often fill the history books. Social change is harder to grasp than technological change: steam engines and automobiles fix themselves more readily in our minds than "increased mobility" or "erosion of natural community." Nevertheless, it is at the level of alterations in ordinary life that modernization has brought about some of its most profound changes. And it is changes at this level that greatly determine the degree of ease or difficulty which most people experience in living out the gospel faithfully and fully.

Social Change: The Key Elements

The story of the coming of the modern world is a story of the draining away of human energies and loyalties from established patterns of association. Cities attract people away from the countryside and its ancient ways of life. Factories, offices, schools, and military forces draw individuals away from the family plot of land or workshop. Thus the last two centuries have seen the collapse or weakening of all the old social structures which used to support marriage, traditional morality, relationships among relatives and neighbors, and the rearing of the next generation in the values of the parents. Because Christianity was enmeshed with the traditional European cultures, this weakening of structures has undermined *Christians'* marriages and sexual morality, *Christians'* relationships of mutual support, and the handing on of *Christians'* way of life to their children.

The stripping away of the structures which supported the mass of people in Christian living is a very complex process. Among its leading features are these:

1. *The enormous enlargement of the scope of life.* In the traditional world there were no large factories or office build-

ings, extensive government bureaucracies or large standing armies. With few even moderate-sized cities, most people lived in villages or hamlets.

The replacement of this tiny-scale world with our metropolitan, global world has affected Christian living at several points. For instance, in the small, preindustrial communities of the traditional world, people held common standards of behavior, and their lives were so intertwined that they were able to know whether all the members were living by community norms and motivated to correct those who were not. Those who strayed—failing to support needy relatives, abusing their wives or children, drinking excessively, or deviating from sexual standards—could be found out and pressured to conform. The anonymity and privacy of metropolitan life frees us from this kind of supervision and leaves us much more on our own to do what is right.

In their small communities, our ancestors had to conduct relationships with far fewer people than we do, and most of the people they dealt with were well-known to them and held common views on the rightness (and inevitability) of the social order and its value system. By contrast, we relate constantly to large numbers of people—school friends, teachers, workmates, bosses, employees, strangers in business transactions, neighbors, experts, the teachers and coaches of our children, and on and on. To be an effective Christian in all these relationships requires a higher, more sophisticated level of training and wisdom than our ancestors needed. Furthermore, in a world full of competing views it requires a greater effort to hold our faith and pass it on to our children. We must maintain the conviction that Christianity is the absolute truth in a world which suggests by its very pluralism that every way must be only relatively true.

2. *The removal of economic activity from the home.* In the small-scale, preindustrial world, most people labored in a family setting—their own or someone else's—growing food, plying a trade, providing personal service. The economies of traditional societies were made up of large numbers of very small units of production.

As a unit of production, the traditional family had a different character from the modern family. For example, while personal attraction played a part in courtship (relatively few marriages were arranged without any consideration of the partners' wishes), economic interests played a heavy part and, after marriage, bound the spouses together. Today, in deciding who to marry, people give most weight to romantic attraction; the question has become, "Are we *really* in love?" Further, in the last two decades, romantic attraction has been overshadowed by erotic expectations. Canadian social historian Edward Shorter comments that the more intense focus on the erotic in many couple's lives "has injected a huge chunk of high explosive into their relationship. Because sexual attachment is notoriously unstable, couples resting atop such a base may be easily blown apart. To the extent that erotic gratification is becoming a major element in the couple's collective existence, the risk of marital dissolution increases."[2]

Not only has the family in modern society ceased to be the unit of production, it has also ceased to be the sphere in which most women spend most of their time. In growing numbers, women are opting to work away from the home. This gives them financial independence, which in turn makes them less hesitant to leave a marriage which proves emotionally unsatisfying. Thus, no longer undergirded by economic considerations, Christian marriages must come to be founded on other bases.

The diminished economic function of the family also deeply affects child rearing. Parents no longer supervise children for as many hours each day as formerly. An important component of parental training—preparation for entry into the world of work—is subtracted from the parent-child relationship. Moreover, the children now have many avenues to success open to them that lie outside the family. Children are no longer reliant on their father for access to their adult station in life, because for most there is no family farm or business to inherit. A reinforcement of the father's authority is thus removed.

3. *The escape from poverty.* While not everyone in modernized societies is free of physical want, modernization in its

advanced forms has for the first time in history made it possible
for the mass of people to escape the acute fear of being poor at
some time in their lives. After examining traditional England,
historian Peter Laslett writes, "It is probably best to assume
that at all times before the beginnings of industrialization a good
half of all those living were judged by their contemporaries to be
poor, and their standards must have been extremely harsh."[3]

Except for extreme situations, in which large numbers of
people were starving (which Laslett believes was uncommon in
traditional England), poverty in the past fostered interdependence. In the traditional small-scale, family-centered world,
widespread physical want reinforced the Christian principle of
love of neighbor. British historian Michael Anderson writes of
the Irish in the early 19th century, before the advent of
industrialization there: "The willingness of the Irish to share
their poverty with others even worse off than themselves was
proverbial, and applied both to kin and non-kin. . . . As an
explanation of why neighbors so willingly gave help to those
with no relatives, one Irish witness said, 'They think that the
potatoes they have are God's, and that when one of his creatures
is in distress, he has as good a right to a share of them as
themselves.' Several Irish witnesses referred to the obligation to
assist kin as a 'sacred one' and 'a religious duty,' one adding,
showing clearly the importance of tradition of this kind in these
closed communities, 'it is the law of the country to do so,' while
another in the same vein said that 'the law of custom holds so
strongly.' "[4]

The escape from poverty has been accompanied by a casting
off of obligations to kin and neighbors. People have taken
advantage of the opportunity to lead lives free of community
supervision and mutual responsibility. Independence being
possible, people have chosen independence. The economic
factor which once reinforced Christian interdependence has
thus been removed, and different dynamics must now come
into play if Christians are to seriously share their lives with one
another at a practical level.

4. *The extension of universal education and the mass communi-*

cations media. In the traditional world, few people had access to knowledge of events before their own time or outside their own small community. In the Christian West, this put the churches in a unique position. Laslett writes, "At a time when the ability to read with understanding and to write much more than a personal letter was confined for the most part to the ruling minority, in a society which was otherwise oral in its communications, the preaching parson was the great link between the illiterate mass and the political, technical, and educated world. Sitting in the 10,000 parish churches of England every Sunday morning in groups of 20, 50, 100, or 200, the illiterate mass of the people were not only taking part in the single group activity which they ordinarily shared with others outside their own families. They were informing themselves in the only way open to them of what went on in England, Europe, and the world as a whole. The priesthood was indispensable to the religious activity of the old world, at a time when religion was still of primary interest and importance. But the priesthood was also indispensable because of its functions in social communication."[5]

The development of mass literacy, and the superceding of literacy by the universally accessible electronic media, have presented the churches with tremendous competition. Other ways of looking at the world, other models of how to live, are now communicated to people powerfully and directly. In a way that was unnecessary in the past, Christians need to be trained to handle the countless varied inputs they receive through the educational and communications systems and to assess the messages from a Christian point of view.

These four points by no means exhaust the list of fundamental ways in which our world is different from the world that has disappeared in the West. We have moved from a world in which individual lives were short, but inherited ways were age-old and were perceived as virtually unchangeable. We have left behind a world in which the great majority of people had very limited choices and prospects of material advancement. We have forgotten the emotional patterns that accompanied the social roles and community life of our ancestors. We have lost one world, and gained another.

In the lapidary expression of American sociologist Marion J. Levy, Jr., "Modernization is a universal social solvent."[6] Its inexorable stripping away of structures that used to support people in patterns compatible with Christianity is one of the great problems facing the churches. The challenge is to develop a full range of responses that will take up the role played by the small communities of the past, and by the former binding force of sheer economic necessity in village and family life. Church life was once one element of a social matrix which to a considerable degree fostered Christian living. That matrix has now been shattered. Christians must find new ways to bring men and women to a firmer and clearer commitment to be disciples of Christ, new ways to structure Christian community life, new environments to support people in leading Christian lives, more practical teaching and training for Christian living.

To say all this is not to idealize the past. We may ask to what extent Christianity penetrated the minds and hearts of most of our ancestors. The supports which the traditional world offered to Christian living did not guarantee genuine Christian life. Stable marriages were not always happy ones. Personal conflicts in the family and village were not always resolved peacefully; bitterness sometimes outweighed forgiveness. The poverty and oppressiveness of the traditional world were considerable. When our ancestors had the opportunity to choose more privacy, more education, more opportunities for social advancement and greater material well-being, they did so, and most of us would ratify their choices. But the point is that, however flawed, the traditional world did provide social supports for Christian living which have now been eroded. Whatever view we take of traditional life, it is gone, and we must find new ways of structuring and sustaining Christian life.

In the present volume, the contributions of Peter Williamson and Mark Kinzer are especially directed toward this goal. Mr. Williamson offers a pastoral description of behavioral changes that indicate Christians' loss of a distinctive way of life, and he locates one cause of this in the ways that modern social structures form a separate world for youth which makes the transference of Christianity to the younger generation difficult. Mr. Kinzer proposes certain pastoral structures as especially helpful in dealing with contemporary social breakdown.

The De-Christianization of Culture

In the modern period, Christians must not only deal with the erosion of social structures but also overcome a shift in the prevailing values of Western societies. Christianity, which once furnished the assumptions, standards, and ideals for intellectual, political, economic, and artistic life in the West, has been swept aside. It is now overshadowed by a secular culture which to some extent it gave rise to. This de-Christianization strips away cultural and legal reinforcements for the Christian approach to marriage, parental authority, sexuality, and so on. In this way it alters the environment in which Christians move. The process of de-Christianization has been very complex, with antecedents in the rediscovery of the pagan classics in the Renaissance and the rationalism and optimism of the Enlightenment, and the secularist views of human nature that these developments fostered. However, three observations are especially pertinent here.

The first observation is that the fragmenting of Western Christendom undoubtedly played an important role in secularization. It is a familiar point that the sequel to the religious wars of the 16th and 17th centuries was, in much of Europe, a dampening of religious fervor, a reduction of religion to formal observance, the acceptance of a bland religion stressing ethical behavior and depreciating doctrine. This style of church life was certainly ill-prepared to master the challenges of either the scientific revolution or industrialization. And so, indirectly, the division of Christendom played a part in the de-Christianization of intellectual life and of much of the working class in modern Europe. However, a less familiar but equally important relationship may be traced between the division of

Christendom *itself*—aside from the destruction that accompanied it—and the secularization of Western life. British historian Christopher Dawson makes this point:

> The chief cause of the secularization of Western culture was the loss of Christian unity—the dissolution of the community in which the peoples of the West had found their spiritual citizenship. The mere fact of this loss of unity created a neutral territory which gradually expanded till it came to include almost the whole of social life. The wars of religion and the long controversy concerning religious toleration, which produced such a prolific literature during the seventeenth century, especially in England, forced men to accept at least as a practical necessity, the principle of common political and economic action by men who differed in their theological views and in their ecclesiastical allegiance; and when once men had admitted the principle that a heretic could be a good citizen (and even an infidel could be a good man of business), they inevitably tended to regard this common ground of practical action as the real world, and the exclusive sphere of religion as the private world, whether of personal faith or merely private opinion.[7]

Dawson's remark leads to a *second observation* on the de-Christianization of Western culture. The process has not gone as far as it has because Christianity has been intellectually discredited. Christianity in the modern age is as intrinsically true and believable as it was in the time of the Roman Empire or at the height of the Middle Ages. Indeed it now has at its disposal an immense theological and intellectual tradition which it did not have when Paul was making the rounds of the cities of Asia and Greece. For various reasons, however, modernization has tended to diminish Christianity's relevance and plausibility in many people's eyes. The sphere of common economic and political activity separate from explicit faith and church connections, which Dawson noted, has continued to grow, not only as a practical necessity due to the shattering of

Christendom but also through the emergence of massive new political and economic institutions. Modern cities, national bureaucracies, corporations, labor unions, school systems, and the rest have appeared. The churches find themselves pushed to the periphery of society by this expansion. In this new technological order, Christianity seems of questionable importance to some, who look to science, technology, and government to answer questions or solve problems.

At the same time, the impressive growth of technology has strengthened the temptation to place man, his accomplishments and his potential, at the center of all consideration. For many people, the transcendent dimension of life becomes excluded from view not so much deliberately as unconsciously. The assumption that the meaning and criteria of all human actions are to be found in this life alone seems to have become accepted to an especially high degree by men and women in the fields of education and communication, with the result that secular humanistic views, which might once have been held by a rather small elite, are now spread abroad to everyone.

In the modern period, then, the secular humanistic outlook draws strength from new sources—the displacement of the churches from a central role in society, the enormous elaboration of the manmade environment, and mass education and popular communication. This is not to say that modernization leads inevitably to secularization, but that what has in fact happened in the modern period is that Christianity has lost the initiative in Western societies.

This leads to a *third observation.* Christians, having lost the initiative in cultural life and exercising progressively less influence on social policies and institutions, have themselves become increasingly susceptible to molding by the secularized societies they live in. This is the subject examined in various ways by three contributors in the present book—James Hitchcock, Harold O.J. Brown, and Ralph C. Martin.

The British evangelical writer Os Guinness has pointed out that in the modern world Christians tend to fall into one of two traps. The first is to allow their religion to become privatized, unapplied to the world of industry, commerce, education, and government. The second is to attempt to penetrate the public world, but in the process to adopt secular models of action and to identify Christianity with secular political ideologies of the left or right. Guinness notes that this problem is rooted in the severe dichotomy between private and public life that modern-ization has effected.[8]

Catholic historian James Hitchcock has identified the crucial role of affluence in nurturing the de-Christianization of Christians in advanced modern societies. He observes that the substitution of "self-actualizing" Christianity for "self-sacrificing" Christianity could not be occurring on a large scale if there were not many people with the means to invest generously in their own self-development. Self-actualization, after all, can be expensive.[9]

American sociologist Peter Berger has perceptively examined Christian theologians' fundamental choice of a secular outlook as a common cognitive response to modernity. He has analyzed how in the writing of various contemporary theologians one can observe a mindset that does not so much quarrel with the supernatural dimension of Christianity as ignore it. The transcendent, eternal aspects of the Christian message become a matter of indifference. Secularism enters theology not so much as a contention but as an assumption.[10]

To sum up, the division of Christendom contributed to the de-Christianization of the West and left the churches unpre-pared to deal with the wrenching transformations of modern-ization. Furthermore, as Christianity lost its ascendency in Western culture the churches, having emerged from the traditional Christendom situation unaccustomed to drawing sharp lines between Christianity and the surrounding culture, were themselves vulnerable to de-Christianizing influences. Just as Christian influences formerly flowed into every aspect of culture, now non-Christian cultural influences began flowing freely into the churches.

This analysis indicates the need for three complementary movements among Christians. The first is that, as the dividing of Christendom was important for the de-Christianization of the West, progress toward Christian unity will be important if Christians are to counter and reverse this trend. This progress is necessary not only among Christians in the West, but also between Christians of the East and West. Some practical thoughts in this direction are offered in this book by Stephen Clark. Second, Christians of all theological traditions need to join in reasserting their faith in the fundamental truths of Christianity which they hold in common and which have been especially undermined in the modern period. This has not yet happened. Rather, various groups of Christians have tended to react separately to what can actually be seen as common modern theological challenges.

For example, in the early 20th century, Catholics and Protestants reacted against theological movements which they both labeled "modernism." While there were significant differences between the liberal Protestantism that the fundamentalists rejected in the United States and the Catholic modernism of Loisy and Buoniauti, which Pius X condemned, there was also a family resemblance, a common parentage. Kant, who denied that reason, used in a speculative or theoretical way, can gain true knowledge of suprasensible things, influenced both Protestant and Catholic modernists in their loss of confidence in the value of dogma based on divine revelation. Schleiermacher, who propounded the view that religion consists essentially in the intuition of radical dependence and reverence, provided both Protestant and Catholic modernists with a way of seeing scripture and Christian doctrine as the record of men's religious experience rather than the authoritative revelation of God's mind. The spirit of both Protestant and Catholic modernism sought reconciliation with modern science, put faith mainly in empirical knowledge, looked for natural rather than supernatural accounts of reality, and replaced the Bible and the church with the individual as the locus of authority. Yet the reaction against the tendencies of modernism did not lead to cooperation between Protestants and Catholics. (Modernism did elicit some alliances among Protestants, however. For instance, the publication of *The Fundamentals* from 1910-1915 represented cooperation between those who strongly held millenialist views, Presbyterians who espoused traditional Calvinism, and others.)

Looking back on the conflict with modernism, the fundamentalist scholar George Dollar enunciates a principle which Christians today ought to apply to the struggles going on in each other's theological traditions regarding contemporary tendencies to secularize Christian teaching. Dollar distinguishes Fundamentalist from Calvinist views of the atonement of Christ, but while disagreeing with Calvinist theology at this point, he nevertheless recognizes that the modernist attack on basic Christian beliefs in the Presbyterian Church was engineered through a revision of the Westminster Confession in 1903. Dollar writes that "the New Theology among Presbyterians came in through the door of a watered-down Calvinism, the system which had been the backbone of this historic denomination. There was a principle at the center of the situation, namely, the right of Presbyterians to attack the standards of faith; whether we agree with those standards or not is beside the vital issue."[11] Presentday evangelical Protestants might take the same view of much theological conflict in the Catholic Church; for example, Catholic dissent which seems more Protestant but which basically fosters a pervasive secularization of Christian beliefs. Catholics might view more sympathetically the efforts of those evangelicals who upheld the authority of scripture in the struggle over biblical inerrancy.

The need for a joint response by Christians from all traditions to the modern temptations to secularize Christian teaching has been articulated by Reformed theologian Donald Bloesch:

> With the rise of theologies that substitute secular panaceas for the biblical gospel, a confessional situation looms on the horizon. The church needs to confess its faith anew when it is threatened by heresy from within. . . . We must be alert to the fact that new theological issues are increasingly forcing themselves upon us. At the time of the Reformation, both

sides affirmed the transcendence and aseity of God, the deity of Jesus Christ, the divine authority of the Bible, and the miracles of Jesus Christ. But all of these are now being called into question—by both Catholic and Protestant scholars.[12]

Embracing the Challenge of a New Age

Looking at modern social changes and particular patterns of de-Christianization, it is no exaggeration to say that an entire period of human history—and church history—has ended, and another has begun. The last two centuries have altered the churches' relationship to surrounding society as decisively as did the peace of Constantine. Constantine brought an end to what may be considered the first period of Christian history, during which the church experienced intermittent persecution and lived in sharp distinction to surrounding society. He opened the way for the building of Christendom, in which Christianity attempted to establish itself as the central value system and institution of Europe. This imperfect union of Christianity and culture has now been dissolved, and the churches have been propelled into a period in which they confront social disintegration on the one hand and deChristianization on the other.

This new age offers opportunities to the churches. Obviously, the technical resources at the disposal of the Christian mission are greater now than they have ever been—the means of travel and publishing, the electronic media, computors, and so on. Even more importantly, the dislocations of the modern period have wrenched many people from their traditional ways of life, leaving them open to the message of salvation. The imprisoning materialism of much of modern life has awakened a deep spiritual hunger in the hearts of many people throughout the world. Thus the tools of evangelism have never been so sophisticated, and the fields have never seemed so vast or so ripe for harvest.

There are other, less obvious, opportunities. The pluralization of worldviews in modern societies presents Christians with a healthy challenge to true discipleship. As modern Western societies continue to dissolve the supports for Christian living, individual Christians must grow in personal commitment to Christ and in the depth of their Christian convictions. And on a corporate level, as these societies discard their grounding of laws and customs in Judeo-Christian morality, Christians have the opportunity to display the Christian life anew. The distinctiveness and attractiveness of Christian living can be demonstrated in fresh contrast to a secularized society.

At the conference from which this book comes, Catholic ethicist Germain Grisez observed that the very social disintegration of the modern period offers Christianity a historic opportunity. As fundamental elements of social life—marriage, child rearing, sexual morality, basic distinctions between men and women—unravel, Christians must answer questions regarding what structures and principles for human life the Christian message provides. In the past Christianity penetrated societies which already had their own traditional social structures, and it attempted to reshape them in a Christian direction. Now Christians must answer the question to what extent Christianity carries its own principles for basic social order. Just as the crisis over the evangelization of the gentiles in the first century provoked a development in the church's understanding of the nature of the gospel, the modern social crisis can provoke Christians to a deeper understanding of what the Christian revelation teaches about the patterns of human life.

To take advantage of these opportunities, however, the churches need strength and vitality. The churches can carry out the Christian mission only if they maintain the integrity of Christian belief, only if individual members have a strong personal commitment and live out the Christian life successfully, only with unity and the power of the Holy Spirit. Unfortunately, these ingredients are weak or lacking in many contemporary church situations. Throughout the modern period the churches have proven to be vulnerable to the secularization of their beliefs—the "demythologization" of the Christian message, the politicization of the church's mission, the shaping of pastoral work according to norms derived from the secular social sciences. The modern world has marked out a secular road and, one after another, churches and Christian groups have trod it. The mainline Protestant churches were entering on the path by the turn of the century; the Catholic Church has lurched in the same direction in the last two decades; observers such as Francis Schaeffer and Os Guinness see the beginnings of the cycle among evangelicals in recent years.

No simple laws hold for the process: church bodies differ in spiritual vitality, size, cultural background, quality of leadership, etc. But if one looks over the last two centuries, one cannot fail to see the pattern. A steady secularizing wind blows in the modern world, and sooner or later most church bodies and organizations begin to drift in response. And even where Christians do maintain basic beliefs firmly, one often finds today disturbing signs of breakdown in actually living out the gospel.

It is true that portions of the churches appear strong and healthy. When one locates these instances of strength and health, however, a significant pattern begins to emerge, which has been noted by the British evangelical leader Michael Harper, among others. While the First World—the West—is not lacking in vigorous expressions of Christianity, many of the most striking Christian developments today are found in the Second and Third Worlds. In the Second World—the Communist-ruled nations—Christians confront modernity in a totalitarian mode. There secularization is forcible, which creates serious problems for Christians but also makes plain the cleavage between secular thinking and Christian beliefs. In the Second World the structures of society undermine Christian living, but there is absent the affluence and personal freedom which nourish the more extreme forms of social disintegration in the West.

The Third World nations are, by definition, latecomers to the processes of modernization. They are trying to make modernization their own but, at present, large parts of these societies are "underdeveloped," which is to say, not yet modernized. And, as all premodern societies (especially those which have begun to secure some of the benefits of modernity, such as medicine, without other benefits, such as increased productivity), they are poor. So Christians in these countries face a range of situations different from those of Christians in the First World.

But the Third World nations are committed to the attempt to modernize. Many Third-World nations are undergoing uneven and traumatic modernization, especially in their rapidly growing cities. To the degree that Third World nations do modernize, we may expect to see Christians in those places having to deal with the problems of social decay and secularized thinking which have so far accompanied the process in the West.

There are reasons to see a climax in certain lines of development in our own day. In the West, the social unravelling which has undone the social hierarchy, the guilds, and the kinship systems of the traditional world has now reached the irreducible unit of society—the nuclear family. The sexual revolution of the 1960s and 1970s has brought to a culmination the breakup of traditional sexual mores and the removal of social supervision which began in the 18th century. This disintegration of the social order cannot logically have much farther to go. In the Second World, Christianity faces a brutally hostile environment. Faith in Marxism has receded in the Communist nations; as Karol Wojtyla noted before becoming pope, "Marxism in the West is still a vehicle for ideas; in the East it is only a vehicle for power."[13] This has left two vast systems—one European, one Asian—both marked by a deadeningly materialistic and efficient totalitarianism. Elsewhere, in much of the Third World, leftist revolutionaries and privileged elites vie for control amid explosive social change.

Strife among family members, sexual immorality, dictatorial intentions, massive economic injustices—none of these are new on the human scene. But at the end of the 20th century these evils have assumed more naked and aggressive forms than ever before. They have at their disposal immensely more sophisticated techniques. The age-old spiritual conflict has come more plainly into view and its tempo has quickened.

Amid disintegration of basic relationships and morality, we might experience the temptation which the psalmist felt: "Fly like a bird to the mountains. . . . If the foundations are destroyed, what can the righteous do?" (Ps 11:1, 3) But our response must be founded on the Lord's promise not to leave us orphans but to send the Holy Spirit to us to declare to us the truth and "the things that are to come." If we truly believe that God continues to speak to his people, we *must* believe that he has something to say to us about the crisis we face. Believing this, our first priority is to turn to him, to submit ourselves to him anew, to listen to him in whatever ways he wishes to guide us.

As individuals we need to grow in faith and in a practical knowledge of how to identify and cooperate with the initiatives and empowerment of the Holy Spirit. We need courage to make radical adjustments in our manner of life and Christian service. Collectively we need to cooperate in efforts to understand the pastoral and intellectual challenges of the modern world. We need to learn new pastoral strategies, especially those that foster lasting spiritual renewal—the subject of James Packer's contribution to this book. We need to renew our submission to the authority of God's word and give a clearer definition to the boundaries of Christian belief and morality. To accomplish these personal and collective goals, there must be a united effort of Christians from throughout the churches who will put themselves to these tasks, placing themselves at God's disposal for his purposes at this hour in history.

Kevin Perrotta
The Center for Pastoral Renewal

ONE

Self, Jesus, and God: The Roots of Religious Secularization

James Hitchcock

A S THE SECOND CHRISTIAN MILLENIUM draws to a close, the religion of Christ, at least as it exists in the United States, manifests a striking pattern, one which could perhaps not be duplicated at any previous time in its history.

On the one hand, there is a resurgence of Christian belief and practice at the popular level, often among people who seemed totally secularized only a few years ago. A story which has not yet found its great confessional voice is that of the many young people, products of the counterculture of ten years ago, who have found their way to faith. Certainly the veritable explosion of primarily evangelical Christianity is one of the most significant events of the 1970s, although predictably those whose business it is to perceive "trends" did not notice this one until it was in full development.

On the other side there is no doubt that much of organized Christianity is also in steady and even rapid decline, judged first by available statistics about church membership and attendance in the so-called "mainline" denominations, and even more by the unmeasurable but nonetheless palpable confusion and erosion of faith which has occurred in those same churches among many of the people who still attend them.

The starkness of the latter fact can hardly be underestimated. I venture to suggest that there is no single Christian belief which, over the past twenty years, has not been challenged, questioned, or denied by respectable people within the mainline churches, people who in most cases have not thereby lost their respectability. It is bemusing to recall that James A. Pike's fellow Episcopal bishops once considered trying him for heresy. Today it is likely that a good proportion of the bishops share much of his perspective.

Depending on which set of present trends one considers, it is possible therefore to predict an America of the year 2000 which is either wholly secular, where Christians have been reduced to a rather odd minority, or one in which a great and permanent religious revival has taken place.

There are elements of this society which have been highly secularized for a long time, groups which seem disproportionately represented in what can be broadly called the communications industry, including education. However, the crisis of unbelief which is now most threatening is less the influence outright secularists may have as the rapid loss of faith among Christians themselves. Such an occurrence is doubly destructive because so often counterfeits of faith are offered as the real thing, and people become secularized without realizing what is happening to them.

Since there is virtually no aspect of Christian belief and teaching which is not now under attack, the catalogue could be endless. I intend to discuss briefly three primary areas: personal morality, the doctrine of Christ, and belief in a personal God. The problems with respect to these areas could be multiplied and extended into most other areas of church life.

It is also worth noticing that the crisis exists on two levels. On one level there are doubts directed explicitly at proclaimed Christian doctrines. On another these same doctrines are undermined often by unrecognized assumptions which are ultimately incompatible with Christian belief.

Sexual Morality

Sexual morality may seem like the dead horse which orthodox Christians have flogged once too often, but it remains central to any consideration of the health of the church, for many important reasons. One of the most important is precisely the intimately personal nature of sexual behavior. Many people can accept the idea of the church judging their social actions, but they resist feverishly the idea that religion can enter into their personal lives. Thus sexual morality remains an important test of a Christian's acceptance of God's authority.

There is also no doubt that sexual morality is the point at which secularists, including secularized church members, have chosen to assault the church's authority, and beyond that any kind of religious authority. The significance of the sexual revolution lies less in what people actually do, whether they violate chastity now more than they used to, than in how they regard what they do. Previously people could lead very sinful lives but do so with a knowledge of their sins and at least the possibility of repentance. But the point of the moral revolution of our time is precisely to teach people how to follow their desires in good conscience and not allow themselves to fall under judgment for anything they do.

Hence the importance of the sexual revolution extends beyond the intrinsic importance of sexual actions. For it is in the area of sexuality that Christians now learn to exalt their own consciences, however flawed or insensitive, into the only working moral absolute. It is a lesson which can be, and is being, applied to every other area of morality.

If we understand the reasons for this fact we will move a long way towards understanding the broader roots of secularization in the modern West. Standard sociological explanations point to the general phenomenon of modernity, especially industrialization, as making secularization virtually inevitable. But it is worth noting that the United States remained a strongly religious nation long after the advent of industrialization and that its rapid secularization has coincided roughly with the beginnings of its industrial decline. Rather than the fact of industrialization itself, some of its long-term fruits may be seen as the chief causes of secularization, especially the prolonged prosperity which America enjoyed for a generation following World War II. Put simply, Americans began to expect unlimited gratification from life. At first this was primarily material. However, habits of expectation developed in one area inevitably spread to others. Americans became increasingly unwilling to accept no as an answer to any of their desires. Just as traditional notions, many of them religious in origin, about the virtues of frugality and simplicity of life were discarded as the excess baggage of a poorer time in history, so traditional ideas about human behavior in general were similarly laid aside. Americans began to conceive it as their birthright to experience a full range of "self-fulfillment." As any competent Christian spiritual director could have foreseen, the search for self-fulfillment is endless and endlessly frustrating. Once embarked upon, it requires at a minimum the rejection of all those things which seem to obstruct that individual's fulfillment. For many people the church has been among the first of these, although clergy frequently rush in to reassure the world that *their* church at least supports personal liberation rather that opposes it.

In the long run it is the family which of all human institutions has suffered most as a result of the sexual revolution. Although commitment to the family and a certain conservatism in sexual matters are perceived by everyone as accompanying one another, it is less often recognized to what extent the sexual revolution is simply a repudiation of the family. In essence, the revolution is a claim to be allowed to experience the satisfactions of sex apart from the context of permanent and committed love, which is marriage. Within marriage the revolution implies both a sundering of sexuality from God's creative purposes and the absolutizing of sexual satisfaction in such a way that married people can, if necessary, look for it outside their marriage. Finally, it requires that supposedly permanent and even sacramental commitments be dissolved when they fail to produce as much satisfaction as the individual feels entitled to.

Obviously, sexual adventuring is not the only or perhaps even the chief cause of divorce in our time, and this illustrates how the sexual revolution is merely the most visible part of a much broader kind of revolution, based on the ideal of total self-fulfillment. It has been pointed out that the great middle class in the United States seems willing to accept almost any degree of discipline, and to make almost unlimited commitments, for the sake of money and careers. Quite possibly, business and professional people today work harder than did their predecessors. But such a willingness to sacrifice is a classic example merely of deferred gratification, forgoing smaller pleasures now for the sake of larger ones later. What the present generation has great difficulty accepting is the concept of truly unselfish living, for the sake of God or the sake of other people. The lust for sexual gratification is part of this, but a much larger part is the unwillingness to make truly binding commitments either to spouses or to children for fear that they will eventually inhibit one's freedom.

No one raised amidst even the remnants of Judeo-Christian morality in the West can embrace such an ethic with a wholly serene conscience, and it is this fact which explains the ferocity of the contemporary moral revolution, its almost compulsively antireligious aggressions. Attempts are being made to secularize society in very radical ways, because those whose consciences are not altogether peaceful in their repudiation of traditional morality want to draw, as it were, a larger and larger circle of immunity around themselves, organizing a kind of conspiracy in which each person tacitly agrees not to condemn anyone else's immorality so as not to be condemned in turn.

No mistake would be more damaging than to assume that this situation is merely a confrontation between proclaimed religious believers on the one hand and proclaimed secularists on the other. It is precisely the influence of secularism *within* the churches which makes the present situation so perilous.

In a paper delivered at the predecessor of this conference I suggested various ways in which the churches have often unwittingly secularized themselves, starting from premises which are correct from a Christian standpoint, but falling into fatal misinterpretations of those premises. Three aspects of this process might be briefly recalled here.

One is misplaced compassion, or rather a misunderstanding of compassion, whereby the delicate line between love of the sinner and love of the sin is disastrously crossed. Discourse in the contemporary church has been skewed in such a way that compassion for the sinner is now understood by many people as necessarily involving acceptance of, or at a minimum a "nonjudgmental" stance towards, the sin. The roots of this go deep, because it is not only a kind of sentimentality and flabby-mindedness masquerading as Christian love, it also calls into play the desire of all of us to escape judgment for our own sins, as part of the moral conspiracy referred to previously.

A second fatal error is a misunderstanding of the requirements of evangelization. Many contemporary Christians sincerely believe that the only way they can reach the unbeliever is by presenting the church's most tolerant face, proclaiming in every way possible that Christianity is now a religion which no longer teaches dogmatically and which no longer pronounces moral judgments with authority. Empirical evidence shows that such a strategy does not bring skeptics to belief. At best it causes them to look on the church with less suspicion, but without any disposition to take it seriously. As numerous studies have shown, it is precisely those denominations which are least compromising in their demands on people which are attracting the most converts. Most often it seems as though the determination to be "open" to skeptics reflects less a desire to win converts than an attempt by the secularized Christian to accommodate his own religious doubts.

The third potentially fatal error is the desire to achieve modernity. In principle this is, once again, legitimate. In every age the church has, whether consciously or unconsciously, developed forms which reflect the world in which it is incarnated and which help make it credible to that world. But modernity of the late twentieth century precisely includes secularity as one of its principal components, which renders such accommodation extremely difficult. In addition, it is often sought in an uncritical and even rote fashion by simply taking over whatever seems influential in modern culture (e.g., Marxism or humanistic psychology) and proclaiming this compatible with Christianity. Most ominously, these secular movements (e.g., feminism) are not infrequently employed as absolutes by which the church itself is judged and continuously found wanting.

In sum, the crisis of contemporary Christianity goes a great deal deeper than disagreement with this or that traditional teaching, or even than whole areas of that teaching, like sex. The ultimate demand of the secularized individual, even if a nominal Christian, is absolute personal moral autonomy, freedom from even the possibility of authoritative judgment pronounced on the self. Attempts by the church to mollify this demand usually have the opposite effect, while paradoxically a firmness of purpose in the same regard often makes the church more credible even in the eyes of the skeptic.

The Doctrine of Christ

There is no doubt that orthodox Christian belief is now being attacked on virtually all fronts, and inevitably the doctrine of Christ is central in this. Apart from the simple stance of rebellious skepticism itself, there is a unity which underlies these attacks, tying together such apparently disparate areas as sexual morality and Christology.

Superficially, there seems to be an upsurge of interest in, even of devotion to, the person of Jesus in recent times, as attested to by the popular musicals *Jesus Christ Superstar* and *Godspell*. However, as orthodox Christians recognize, there are at the very least certain ambiguities in this renewed interest. To begin with, much of it obviously involves a desire to have Christ without Christianity. There is a tradition, dating back at least to the Enlightenment of the eighteenth century, which professes to reverence Jesus but to believe that his disciples and later followers corrupted his teaching. As sinners, Christians are indeed always prone to corrupting that teaching. However, what the world regards as corruption is often likely to be fidelity, and vice versa.

Christians are sometimes accused of having a proprietary attitude towards Christ, as though he were their possession, whereas, it is argued, his lordship over the universe obviously must transcend the narrow boundaries of the church. There is another dimension here, however. Organized Christianity aims to preserve Christ's teaching through time and space, to make it real and powerful in each generation. Whatever else it is, the church is an objective and solid reality which the individual, as it were, must bump against.

The churchless Christ of our contemporaries is intended to be a free-floating figure of the imagination, an image which the individual can share and fashion at will. In much of contemporary popular Christology it hardly matters whether Jesus was a real historical being at all, so long as his image remains powerful. Thus he is variously turned into a political agitator, a clown, a kindly elder brother, a kind of therapist, even (as the marriage feast at Cana is now often interpreted) as a sort of easygoing hedonist.

In a sense it can be said that contemporary Christology is an effort to cut Jesus down to size. Secularized modern people, including some Christians, are uncomfortable with the Christ who is a divine person. They want a Jesus who is companionable, kind, and supportive, and who nevers threatens judgment, never enjoins them to become better than they are.

In this connection it is remarkable how Christ's miracles have been all but defined out of existence in much of contemporary Christianity. The valid assertion that the miracles were not intended as proof of divinity but as manifestations of it to those who already believed, has been subtly reinterpreted to mean almost that the miracles were the subjective experiences of his followers, not corresponding to any verifiable reality. So too the Jesus who spoke with piercing and sometimes peremptory authority has almost entirely given way to a Jesus who seems almost like a tolerant therapist.

Modern biblical scholarship has of course played an indispensable role here, since most often powerful passages in the New Testament which strongly affirm Christ's divinity are dismissed as the interpolations of the church. It is difficult for the non-specialist to judge the adequacy of such claims, but it is at least worth noticing that, like all scholarship, biblical research is not pursued in a social and cultural vacuum. There are at least grounds for a certain suspicion when the findings of scholarship seem so consistently to undermine precisely those beliefs which are incredible to the contemporary secularized mind.

Historically, almost all Christological heresies have stemmed from an inability to believe that Jesus could have been both God and man. Perhaps most commonly, in the early church, this took the form of a denial of his humanity. In modern times it is much more common to deny his divinity. But an important new element has entered. Earlier Christological heresies usually stemmed out of faulty metaphysical speculation, genuine intellectual perplexities about very difficult concepts. Today it is obvious that many people are simply uncomfortable with the divine Jesus. If they truly accepted him as the second Person of the Trinity incarnate, it would make a radical difference in the way in which they would have to view themselves and their relationship to him.

Belief in a Personal God

With respect to belief it is worth observing how what might be called the "high" theology of God—developed in metaphysical categories over so many centuries—has fallen into neglect even among theologians. Certainly it is the rare pulpit from which any preaching about God in and of himself, as distinct from his relations with humanity, takes place.

Once again more is involved here than simply a cultural distaste for metaphysics. For to attempt to plumb the vastness of God in the classical manner would be to realize immediately the vast gulf which separates man from God, and this too the modern mind finds uncongenial, because it seems to threaten the fragile and laboriously built up kind of humanism which is fundamentally incompatible with authentic Christianity.

There are those Christians who point out, sometimes with considerable sharpness, that man's ideas are not necessarily the same as God's. But in our time this valid reminder is almost always issued in order to assert that God is more permissive than man, that what man condemns as sin God accepts and perhaps even approves.

John Calvin was not the first Christian to point out that man's notions of justice are not those of God. But Calvin's version of that insight leads to the assertion that God is less "compassionate," as the world understands compassion, than is man. Once the separation between human and divine ideas of justice has been made, Calvin's version is at least as compelling as that of modern sentimentalized humanism.

That such humanism has become semi-official in advanced Christian circles reveals how God also, like his Son, is now often treated primarily as an idea in the mind, an image in the imagination, rather than a really existing being. The neglect of the metaphysical theology of God stems not only from an aversion to contemplating the gulf between man and God but also from a disinterest in, even sometimes a distaste for, considering God as he is. The contemporary mind wants to be free to mold God into whatever image seems useful and appropriate at a given moment. (The fashion of referring to God as "she" is the most obvious example.)

There is an odd irony in the fact that so much of modern theology (think of Bishop John Robinson) has chipped away at what it regards as human beings' overly anthropomorphic concept of God—an elderly man with a white beard who is "up there." Yet what has replaced these traditional popular ideas, whatever they may have been, seems to be most often a concept of God as a kindly, indulgent grandfather (or grandmother), someone who "understands" me when other people say I have done wrong. The notion seems extremely widespread in the contemporary world, among both church members and non-church members, that, if the individual believes he or she is right, then God thinks so too. There is, perhaps, an unconscious acknowledgement here that God is treated merely as a projection of the self.

A very high percentage of people admit to believing in a personal God, a much higher percentage than are affiliated with any church. A staple of contemporary culture is the individual (for example, Dolly Parton) who admits to being deeply religious but also to having no use for churches. As with the churchless admirers of Christ, a central part of this is the desire to be free precisely to reshape one's image of God in whatever way one chooses. Churches are bothersome because, unless wholly secularized, they still insist on at least some objective realities about God, and they proclaim a relationship of the individual to God which is one of humility and submission.

Underlying all of the contemporary religious crisis, and rarely discussed in its own terms, is belief in divine revelation. Here it is possible to discern an interesting regress that has occurred both in Catholicism and Protestantism. Superficially, modern liberal Catholics have become more biblical. Now every question which arises within the Catholic Church is immediately referred to biblical authority for solution by people who are often willing to bypass everything the church has called tradition—mainly the pronouncements of popes and ecumenical councils, along with the church's very ancient and rich theological store.

But as liberal Catholics are in this sense becoming more Protestant, liberal Protestants are becoming less biblical. There is no doubt that, although it is rarely admitted, certain other "sources" are now accorded at least equal weight with scripture in determining truth, for example, Marxism or modern psychology. In practice the Bible is treated as essentially a human book—profound, inspiring, but nonetheless only human, primarily the record of how people in the Judeo-Christian tradition have understood and interpreted their own "religious experiences." Liberal Catholics have rapidly passed through a phase of what might be called classical Protestant biblicism and have joined their liberal Protestant brethren at this yet more advanced stage.

Christianity, as innumerable commentators have pointed out, is a historical religion, meaning that its central affirmations have to do with human history, in particular that at a certain point in that history the Son of God became man and died. Most other religions of the world cannot comprehend how the infinite could, as it were, be localized. But the scandal goes beyond this. For if the Son of God became man at a particular point in history, then it is also true that God's self-revelation in his Son is extended through history in equally specific ways. Everything which is specific is, or seems to be, limited, and it is this which the modern secular mind cannot accept. Thus many Catholics cannot accept their church's classical understanding of itself because they find the Catholic tradition restrictive. This is not a truly Protestant position, however, since many contemporary Christians, including Protestants, are increasingly embarrassed by the claims to uniqueness of Christianity itself. As such they may be inspired by the Bible, but they cannot help suspecting that it is after all only one sacred book among many.

Given the present tendencies of liberal Christianity, it is inevitable that the name and reality "Christian" will itself by repudiated, for precisely the same reason—as much as people may admire and be inspired by Christ, they will not permit themselves to recognize him as the unique self-revelation of God, the only incarnation of God's Son.

Two streams come together here—the dogmatic cultural relativism of the modern world, which would in principle deny the unique truth of Christianity, and the desire of the modern secularized individual to be free of all constraints on the self. If all religious "revelation" is treated as an expression of the ongoing spiritual search either of individuals or peoples, then it holds no ultimate authority over the self, is indeed merely an emanation of that self.

But one of the purposes of authentic Christianity is to take people out of themselves, to provide them with the means to overcome self-centeredness and distorted self-love. Secularized kinds of Christianity now do the opposite, because they treat spiritual reality not as something objective and infinite but merely as reflecting the depths of the individual's own soul. This self-preoccupation is then justified and the individual is encouraged.

Ultimately, therefore, God himself can only be treated as the deepest dimension of the self, as some contemporary theologies insist. The most fundamental disease of the modern psyche is solipsism, the need for an empty universe to be filled by an infinitely expanding self.

TWO

Faith, Life, and the Spirit of the Age

Harold O.J. Brown

A S A YOUNG CHRISTIAN in college and in seminary, I spent a
couple of years searching the pages of church history for
the original, uncorrupted church. Implicit in the concept
Reformation is the idea that there was once a *formation*. Both
Luther and Calvin—whose writings strongly shaped my early
Christian awareness—intended to recover and to restore something that in their eyes was lost, but not irretrievably so.
Certainly both of them were convinced that a true, pure church
once existed, and could exist again. When Jesus promised, "On
this rock I will build my church" (Mt 16:18), they might be
convinced that church tradition was in error in thinking Peter
and the papacy to be the rock he meant, but they were even
more firmly convinced that there was no mistaking his intention
to build a church. The little Epistle of Jude begins with the
exhortation "that ye should earnestly contend for the faith
which was once delivered unto the saints" (Jude 3). There
was—and is—a church in God's plan, and there was—and is—a
faith once delivered to the saints. And so Luther and Calvin
thought; so, I was and am persuaded, it must have been—and
must still be.

The quest for a pure church, or for a time when the church

was pure, led further and further back into the earliest days of church history—indeed, into the pages of the New Testament itself, in which we find a church troubled with incest (1 Corinthians), with legalism (Galatians), and even with that strange fancy known as Gnosticism (Colossians). There was, evidently, never a time without trouble, indeed, never a time without what the early Christians soon came to call heresy. At first, this was disillusioning for me. Then, with the passage of time, I found a constancy in the variation, a unity in the diversity. And even the exotic ideas of the great heretics revealed themselves as interpretations—misinterpretations, if you will—of a real Jesus Christ, true God and true man. Heresy became a kind of attestation of the fact that there really was—and is—a "faith once delivered," to which men in different centuries react, in an amazingly repetitive way, with ever-fresh "rediscoveries" of the same old misinterpretations and heresies. The recurrence of the distortions attests the reality of the original.

It is possible to follow the image of Christ in the mirror of heresy and orthodoxy through seventeen centuries—from the second into the nineteenth. But at the end of the nineteenth century, and at the beginning of our twentieth, something happens. The old orthodoxy remains—embattled, perhaps, but still vigorous. And the old heresies are still there too; indeed, sometimes a long-quiet one suddenly resurfaces. But somehow the situation is different. Among the early heretics, all parties were convinced of the overwhelming majesty of Jesus Christ—and of the vital importance of knowing and telling the truth about him. Early heretics tried to do too much, tried to explain and to understand things that really exceed our grasp. But they were convinced that there was something of absolutely vital importance there to explain and to understand.

In our own day, we have in every branch of the church those for whom both the old institutions and the old doctrines have become a matter of indifference, even of boredom. They have, in effect, made Pilate's question their motto: "What is truth?" (Jn 18:38). And they do it not in the sense of an inquiry aimed at finding truth, but as a rhetorical question, supposing that truth does not and cannot exist, and appearing persuaded that even if it did it would be of no interest or usefulness. It is not so much as though the old doctrines have been examined, criticized, attacked, disproved, and rejected, as that they have simply been given up as no longer "relevant." "It is simply incomprehensible," they seem to feel, "how anybody can consider the Christian doctrine of redemption as a guide for the difficult life of today."[1] The quotation is from a learned German thinker, but one whom few would want to claim as a spiritual guide—Nazi Propaganda Minister Dr. Joseph Goebbels. The odiousness of the source of this observation should not blind us to the fact that despite the demise of its author and the total destruction of the system of which he was an architect, *this* idea, at any rate, has survived him. For much of our generation, and for many, indeed for all too many, in the churches, Christian doctrine is taken to be irrelevant to the difficult life of today. Heresy exists, and so does orthodoxy—but except for a handful of orthodox, no one is passionate about either. Early heretics were desperately convinced of the rightness of their views and of the wrongness of what our tradition calls orthodoxy. Contemporary people may be convinced of the wrongness of orthodoxy, but they are not at all passionate about whatever heresy they may put in its place. Dramatic changes have taken place, and still are taking place, but they now appear to be seen as part of an organic, evolutionary process, not as an intellectual exercise intended to discover and to demonstrate truth. The consequences for Christian thought and life are profound, even in those circles which, until quite recently, were thought most firmly wedded to the "fundamentals," i.e., among the actual fundamentalists of the old stock, and among their generally similar but somewhat less stiff evangelical cousins.

Doctrine

There are two classic doctrines about which major heresies took shape—the doctrine of God, or, more specifically, of the

Trinity, and the doctrine of Christ, i.e., Christology. The doctrine of the Trinity specified that one God is to be acknowledged as subsisting in three persons, while the doctrine of Christ specifies that one person, Jesus Christ, possesses two complete natures, human and divine. It is not so much that these fundamental and crucial doctrines are denied and disbelieved. They *are* widely disbelieved, and often explicitly denied as well. But far more important is the fact that the center of interest has shifted so far away from them. Classical theology developed the terminology of inward and outward works, of properties and decrees, of communicable and incommunicable divine attributes, in order to attempt, in poor human terms, to come to grips in some way with the divine mystery. Much contemporary theology simply isn't interested. In the churches where there once was a highly developed, highly sophisticated theology and Christology, such as Roman Catholicism and the major orthodox Protestant traditions, the Nicene and Chalcedonian creeds survive, but often—alas!—more as museum pieces than as statements of anyone's actual faith. Fundamentalism and evangelicalism on the whole always fervently believed the great theological and Christological assertions of the creeds, but seldom used the creeds to express them. Thus when fundamentalist and evangelical convictions begin to drift with the tides of time, there is not so ready a reference-point by which to check them and to verify the drift. Nevertheless it is taking place, far less dramatically and devastatingly than in the so-called "mainline" churches of Protestantism, but definitely there.

The Doctrine of Creation

"I believe in God, the Father Almighty, Maker of heaven and earth." So the Apostles' Creed begins; the Nicene Creed says the same thing a trifle more expansively. The idea that God is the absolute Creator, *ex nihilo,* of all that exists, is the presupposition for his authority to order not only the laws of nature but the conduct of human beings. The doctrine of purposeful divine creation has not been refuted, either by science or by philosophy. Indeed, in a real way it cannot be refuted, because all that critical science could tell us, really, is how things might have developed; not having been there as they developed, science can produce at best a probable or very probable hypothesis, but not a direct witness to known facts.

But, as we all know, the doctrine of Creation has been virtually abandoned in the wake of the successful propaganda victory of evolutionism, with the church seldom holding out or even protesting. Protest and counterattacks are left largely to a limited circle of zealots, and more sophisticated evangelicals and orthodox—including a personal friend, author of one of the most celebrated evangelical books of 1981—feel themselves called upon to join the attack on fundamentalism, and through it, on Creation. Thus they place themselves in alliance with organizations such as the American Civil Liberties Union, for whom any creationist alternative to Darwin has become as awful a horror as the prospect of a prayer in a public school.

Because the doctrine of Creation, while not rejected, is being neglected and in a way abandoned in many evangelical Protestant circles, theologically conservative Protestants lack confidence that they can appeal to their fellow-citizens on the basis of shared convictions about natural law, or even about the true meaning of human life. What this means, in practice, is that many contemporary Protestants with strong conservative theological convictions are losing the confidence that they can address themselves to moral and ethical issues that involve the concept of a natural order, of an intrinsic meaning and destiny of human life. Thus issues such as abortion and homosexuality become first embarrassing, then, finally, unapproachable.

From Satisfaction to Liberation

If evangelicalism, while defending the doctrine of Creation in principle, would rather talk about something else, what would it prefer? The answer, of course, is the great doctrine of redemption. The classical approach to the doctrine of redemption, shared by Roman Catholics and by all of the Reformation church—though it is articulated differently by the Eastern Orthodox churches—is that of substitutionary satisfaction. Christ, in the words of the beloved Apostle, "is the propitiation for our sins" (1 Jn 2:2). The concept of propitiation—the satisfaction of the just demands of an offended deity—presupposes the whole edifice of orthodox, Chalcedonian Christology. (Although "monophysite" churches, such as the Armenian Orthodox Church, did not subscribe to Chalcedon, on the points with which we are concerned there was no substantial difference between those churches and the churches that did subscribe.) Christ as man is entitled to represent us, while as God he is able to make a "full, perfect, and sufficient sacrifice." Chalcedonian Christology is not denied; indeed, when challenged and when, if necessary, explained, fundamentalists and evangelicals will affirm it. But they do not emphasize it; the doctrine of the two natures is hard to conceptualize, and it certainly is an impossible subject for a television documentary. But along with the concept of the propitiating, sacrificed Victim we also lose the concept of the propitiated, satisfied Judge. Without a full Christology, satisfaction becomes impossible, and without a fully trinitarian doctrine of God, it is impossible to understand the idea of propitiation. Along with propitiation disappears the idea of the need to reconcile humans with God; what remains is the necessity to reconcile them with one another—perhaps after first taking the precaution of eliminating the irreconcilable elements, the "exploiters." And liberation (in human terms) becomes the new name for salvation.

This development has not yet taken place within evangelicalism; it certainly is at odds with the fundamentals that evangelicals, like fundamentalists themselves, profess. But the ritual of reaffirming the creeds is all but unknown, and even the fundamentals are seldom explicitly restated. The idea of liberation is not substituted for atonement anywhere, but the rhetoric that accompanies it is making inroads. Among evangelicals it has already become popular to speak of exploitation of the oppressed, and of multinational corporations. Each of these themes is important—the last no doubt the least so—and we could cite other slogan-words. In themselves they are important, and not dangerous. But when the rhetoric of liberation enters the language of the evangelical, and when no clear and explicit credal and doctrinal barriers are present to cordon it off, it is not merely possible but virtually inevitable that liberation will soon appear as a more and more acceptable equivalent for satisfaction.

The interesting odyssey of Billy Graham perhaps illustrates that it is in the realm of political applications of the gospel, either of the right or the left, rather than in the realm of doctrine, that evangelicals and fundamentalists are most likely to be brought into contact with the formative power of the spirit of the age. Thirty years ago he was decried and lampooned by liberal Protestants and by the secular media, with notable exceptions. The offensive film *Elmer Gantry* starred Burt Lancaster playing in a way to evoke the Carolina evangelist. A friend of presidents, Graham habitually and vigorously defended the American way of life, capitalism, and national security, so much so that younger admirers, such as I myself was, found it necessary to defend him as merely oversimplifying, but not falsifying the gospel. Shocked by the hypocrisy of some in high office, whom he not merely trusted but seems also to have cultivated, Graham, without discernibly changing his theological convictions, has become a spokesman for nuclear disarmament, for disarmament per se, and at least by implication—he explicitly denies this interpretation of his views—and by faint criticism, spokesman even for the religious settlements imposed on the churches by Communist regimes. The important thing that should be noted here is not that Dr. Graham's theology has changed, but that his applications have. His earlier, naively patriotic views he defended as quite consistent with the gospel, and his present, somewhat different concerns he defends in like manner. Can it be that the gospel itself is a flexible thing which can be pressed into different services, now into that of national security, now into that of nuclear disarmament?

The ground that Graham has vacated on the right of evangelicalism has now been occupied by other forces, led by the redoubtable Jerry Falwell and inspired by the thought of the venerable Francis Schaeffer. I have personal ties to each of these men and would not want to be seen as attacking any one of the three. But is it not possible to say that even Falwell and Schaeffer, as they occupy terrain yielded by Graham, are becoming politicized in a way which—while it may be admirable and indeed, while I myself support it—is rather at odds with the exclusively theological, Christological, and evangelistic approach of their earlier years? Before it changes doctrines, the spirit of the age seems able to modify applications, and the applications, in time, appear to "make ancient good uncouth."

There is a way to exercise an effective Christian witness and ministry to a morally and economically fractured society, and to do so in a way that is consistent with traditional orthodox convictions, indeed in a way that flows from them. But in order to do this, it is necessary to know, to articulate, indeed constantly to rearticulate those convictions, and then to think on them and from them to the applications they require in social and moral areas. This is possible, but it is precisely what the spirit of our age denies. And the theologically conservative Protestant tradition, to the extent that it seeks to placate the spirit of the age by joining with him in areas where he has at least a good claim to justice on his side, is in danger of losing sight of its own foundations.

A Substitution

Early Christianity had battle cries and passwords. Such were the creeds. Contemporary theological conservatism also has a battle cry and a password: the inerrancy of scripture. This is not a popular view; in fact, most of the intellectual community would consider it just as ridiculous as the defense of Adam and

Eve against Darwin. I hold it—lest there be misunderstand-
ings. But—compared with the great affirmations of the unity
of God, of creation, of the Trinity, and of the diety and
humanity of Christ—inerrancy is a narrow plank. It simply is
not broad enough to bear the fullness of the "faith once
delivered" across the centuries and to deposit it safely and
soundly in our own. As J. Robertson McQuilkin, president of
Columbia Bible College, warned years ago, evangelicals and
fundamentalists are in some danger of winning the battle in
defense of inerrancy and yet of losing every good that inerrancy was intended to protect. In an interview to explain
"fundamentalism" some years ago, Dr. Bob Jones II, asked
what fundamentalists believe about abortion, stated, "It is
murder." But when asked what they were prepared to do
about it, Jones replied succinctly, "Nothing." His reasoning
was that political actions by fundamentalists for reason of
Christian principle would violate the separation of church and
state. To defend inerrrancy may be a sound theological policy;
indeed, we believe that it is. But to defend inerrancy, which
the Bible does not require us to do, while at the same time *not*
defending the sanctity of human life, which the Bible does
require, seems a strange way of demonstrating that one has not
tampered with the "faith once delivered."

Life

The New Testament idea of the faith includes but is not
limited to the keeping of right doctrine. It also requires a right
approach to life, right conduct. James tells us, "Faith without
works is dead." Luther, it is true, found fault with this epistle,
and compared it unfavorably to the writings of Paul with his
concept of "justification by faith *alone*" (Luther himself
thoughtfully supplying the word "alone"). But Paul also calls
for active faith, "faith working through love" (Gal 5:6) and tells
his followers, "Be imitators of me" (1 Cor 11:1). If the spirit of
the age has undercut orthodox doctrine, it has not yet so fully
undercut the practice of piety in theologically conservative

Protestant circles. But here too our lack of regularly accepted formal canons of conduct may make it possible for serious problems to arise without being identified and dealt with.

Fundamentalism and Worldliness. The movement that we call fundamentalism has been characterized from the beginning by a rigid concept of the separation of the church from the world, not only in doctrine but in life. Whereas Roman Catholicism, like Eastern Orthodoxy, was very much at home in the highest strata of European society, and German Pietism was at home in the imperial court of the Hohenzollerns, fundamentalism in America has generally been "beyond the pale" socially—partly in reaction to the theological defection of so many intellectually and socially prominent Protestants, partly due to the sociological character of the population groups from which it was recruited. Fundamentalism has on the whole held on very well to its traditional standards of conduct, and has not been embarrassed to defend them in areas where its more sophisticated younger sister, evangelicalism, is uncertain or timid. Thus, after some hesitation brought on by reflections concerning the separation of church and state, fundamentalism has reaffirmed and defended traditional moral standards in an area where most of society has lost them—in matters of sexual morality and in the biomedical areas that relate to sexual conduct, especially with respect to abortion.

Nevertheless, fundamentalism, because it lacks a systematic canon of moral values, may find it hard to set priorities for the defense of its standards—hence the fundamentalists' campaign for prayer in schools is fought with the same intensity as its battle against abortion.

Evangelicalism. Evangelicalism wanted to set itself off from the fundamentalism that preceded it, not by new doctrines but by a new openness to the social dimensions of the gospel. The difference in mentality is suggested by the words fundamental— related to foundations—and evangelical—related to good news. But by the lack of focus on creeds, dogmas, and definitions, evangelicals find themselves vulnerable to infiltration by the spirit of the age in areas of belief and in matters of conduct as well. As Richard Quebedeaux points out in *The Worldly Evangelicals*, some modern evangelicals have learned to be wine connaisseurs. It is not the rediscovery of this once-disdained beverage that is important, but rather the fact that its new acceptability has come about as a matter of taste, not of morals. In other words, evangelicals who once thought that the drinking of wine was wrong came to accept it because they wanted to be "in good taste," not because they were persuaded that their earlier condemnation was not biblically justifiable.

It is in the area of sexual morality that evangelicalism shows the greatest tendency to replace biblical canons of conduct with secular standards of taste. Divorce has made such inroads into evangelical Christian circles that a noted lay leader, a member of one prominent Chicagoland evangelical church, could divorce his wife and marry the "correspondent" in the divorce in another leading evangelical church in the area three weeks later. It is reminiscent of what the British captain said to the Italian colonel in Alberto Sordi's film, *The Best of Enemies:* "Nobody likes war, but you people don't even make the effort." Nobody can really prevent divorce among Christians, but you people don't even make the effort.

Divorce is the rupture of a covenant relationship exceeded in importance in the Bible only by the covenant with God himself. The Bible often compares sexual fidelity with spiritual faithfulness; adultery is a metaphor for idolatry. Where divorce is readily allowed, then premarital chastity can no longer be so central; the acceptance of divorce leads to large numbers of singles in evangelical churches, to a "singles' ministry," and to a situation in which evangelical "singles' fellowships" sometimes seem to be little different from singles' bars, except that no alcoholic drinks are served.

The abandonment of natural law, mentioned earlier, has removed a major barrier to the practice of homosexuality. One evangelical pastor I know, preaching through 1 Corinthians, was advised by two members of his session that they were practitioners of the homosexuality that he said Paul condemned in chapter six. The other members of the session, shocked at first, soon came to accept the homosexual relationship, arguing that the participants demonstrated "fidelity." The preaching of the Word, rather than bringing the hearers under conviction of sin, merely exposed a conflict between teaching and practice, and resulted in the teaching being toned down to fit the practice.

Such a development would have been shocking in the eyes of highly moral liberal Christians such as were most of my teachers at the Harvard Divinity School in the mid-1950s.

In liberalism, one might say that morals outlasted doctrine; the decline of doctrine preceded that of morals. But where evangelicals have insulated themselves from doctrinal decay, moral transformation has nevertheless seeped in, and the decline of doctrine is now following. The current evangelical concentration on inerrancy (for it) and on evolution (against it), while in itself commendable, represents a shift of emphasis away from the most fundamental doctrines of all, such as those of Christology and of the Trinity. It is not that evangelicals in any sense reject or even downgrade them, but rather that they are concentrating on other things. Even more significantly, the concentration on doctrinal issues such as inerrancy is being pursued while important moral problems are being neglected or dealt with in a very superficial manner. It will be a strange thing if we succeed in maintaining the doctrine of inerrancy and in defeating that of evolution while tacitly accepting easy divorce, abortion, and homosexuality.

"But time and chance happeneth to them all" (Eccl 9:11). Conservative Protestantism is still "behind the times" (and thank God that it is so!), but—consciously or unconsciously—it is rushing to catch up. It needs to be turned in a different direction, lest it drift so far that it can never regain the true course. I close with St. Paul's words, "Be not conformed to this world, but be ye transformed by the renewing of your mind" (Rom 12:2).

THREE

The Attack on God's Word— And the Response

Ralph C. Martin

THE CHRISTIAN PEOPLE TODAY are facing many serious challenges to their integrity. I would like to examine four passages in scripture that indicate some of the spiritual forces that are at work in the present situation, passages which identify the problems that God's people face today.

The first passage, Genesis 3:1-6, is a key to understanding the satanic strategy that is undermining God's word. The second passage is Romans 1:18-32, which vividly describes the effects of this satanic strategy on mankind. The third is Luke 19:41-44, which provides us with a glimpse of God's provision for our situation today. The fourth passage is Isaiah 55:6, which guides us to one of the main ways of responding to this situation.

Satan's Strategy for Human Destruction

In John 8:44, Jesus identifies the satanic strategy for destroying the human race. Satan's strategy is clear: he uses lies to lead mankind to death. "The father you spring from is the devil," Jesus tells those who reject him, "and willingly you

49

carry out his wishes. He brought death to man from the beginning, and has never based himself on truth; the truth is not in him. Lying speech is his native tongue; he is a liar and the father of lies." In Genesis 3:1-6, we see this father of lies in action. This passage not only reveals the reason for the fall of the human race, but also the satanic strategy which has operated throughout history and continues today.

> Now the serpent was the most cunning of all the animals that the Lord God had made. The serpent asked the woman, "Did God really tell you not to eat from any of the trees in the garden?" The woman answered the serpent: "We may eat of the fruit of the trees in the garden; it is only about the fruit of the tree in the middle of the garden that God said, "You shall not eat it or even touch it, lest you die." But the serpent said to the woman: "You certainly will not die! No, God knows well that the moment you eat of it your eyes will be opened, and you will be like gods who know what is good and what is bad." The woman saw that the tree was good for food, pleasing to the eyes, and desirable for gaining wisdom. So she took some of its fruit and ate it; and she also gave some to her husband, who was with her, and he ate it.

Satan's first move was to sow doubt in the woman's mind about whether she heard God correctly: Did God really say that? Are you sure you heard him right? Are you sure you properly interpreted his message to you? Are you sure that it was God who said that? By using such tactics, he made the woman experience God's word as narrow and restrictive, keeping her from something that she deserved to have. She lost confidence in God's goodness.

I believe this satanic strategy is at work today in the lives of millions of people, causing them to doubt whether they have heard God correctly, to feel that Christianity is narrow and oppressive, and to believe that the only way to fulfillment in life is to break out of the confinements of God's word and reach out for an autonomy and a fulfillment apart from God. As a result, the lives of millions of people are headed for disaster. Unfortunately, this satanic strategy is also at work in many of the churches. The authority of God's word is being undermined in our midst.

Direct Denial of God's Word

First of all, the power and effect of God's word is being undermined through the direct denial of its authority. Several years ago, I read the text of a convocation address that a prominent professor from a major Protestant seminary in the United States delivered. His words were startling:

What does ancient Christian tradition, with its archaic language and individualistic ethos, have to do with the necessarily social and secular expression of Christianity today? What is the point any more of teaching or studying the classical disciplines when the bases for our action are given with sufficient clarity by contemporary ethics and the adjunct studies of sociology and psychology? I suspect that many of us here, if our back were against the wall, would honestly have to answer, "Very little indeed." We may have some aesthetic interest in tradition, but we are no longer in any danger of confusing aesthetic with normative judgments. There is thus probably a widespread, intuitive acceptance of two affirmations: (1) the New Testament and the creeds are no longer in any way authoritative or canonical for us; (2) the Christian today can find sufficient guidelines for his faith and action in contemporary statements and solutions.

We are thus in no secure place. We have found no single authoritative standard from the past of what to say or how to live. Neither have we a secure self-understanding erected on the basis of our immediate experience. We in fact find ourselves in the abyss of continual uncertainty, but we are kept from falling into chaos by the very tension between past and present. Our specific spot over the abyss is the result of our own individual dialogue. We have no assurance that where we happen to be is the best or final place to stand.[1]

Many of God's people are in an abyss of uncertainty. They no longer know whether they can trust God's word, and, consequently, they do not know where to turn for direction. What a place for God's people to be—cut off from God's word and in an "abyss of continual uncertainty," able to be blown about, as scripture says, by every wind of doctrine!

The direct denial of God's word is not restricted to certain liberal seminaries; it is increasingly becoming an attitude of the ordinary man on the street. A while ago, I read a letter to the editor of a Catholic diocesan newspaper from a housewife who wrote in regard to the regular reading in church of the passage in Ephesians that relates to husbands and wives, parents and children.

> I'm sorry, dear Editor, but I don't believe that the excerpt from Paul to the Ephesians is the word of the Lord; and if believing is living what we believe, neither does anyone else, be they husband or wife! Paul's words are fossils, to be kept in libraries for scholars to read and remark to each other about how primitive people were in "Bible times," how uncivilized. Furthermore, if these readings are so difficult to understand, and their occurrence in our liturgy is the cause of people losing faith, then those people in Rome are saying, "It is better to insist that Paul's words are the word of the Lord and lose souls than it would be to strike Paul's archaic language from the liturgy and use something meaningful in its place."
> . . . The books of the Bible were put together as one book by men; let wiser men take them apart.[2]

It is interesting to read what some of the Fathers of the Church had to say about people who, in their day, took a similar approach to scripture. St. Hippolytus saw only two explana-

tions for the problem: there was either a problem of faith and
unbelief, or a problem of satanic activity.

> They [i.e., people who are undermining the authority of
> God's word] have not feared to lay hands upon the sacred
> Scriptures, saying that they have corrected them. Nor is it
> likely that they themselves are ignorant about how very bold
> their offense is. For either they do not believe that the sacred
> Scriptures were spoken by the Holy Spirit, in which case
> they are unbelievers, or if they regard themselves as being
> wiser than the Holy Spirit, what else can they be but
> demoniacs?"[3]

A couple of years ago, I happened to pick up a copy of a
national Catholic magazine devoted to parish renewal and read
the following from an editorial that issued a ringing call to
abandon God's word and give ourselves to bisexuality.

> Persons—young and old, Hollywood beauty and spiritual
> beauty—have all become sex "objects" for me.
> So why not male and female? . . . .
> The law of God, you say? Come on, let's grow up
> theologically too. We say we don't hold an anthropomorphic
> God, a kind of great puppeteer, old, male (and hetero-sexual
> may one suppose?), so let's really not hold one. No, God
> works the wonders of his providence, of his love, and his laws
> right down inside the concrete, living, *individual* natures he
> creates and sustains.[4]

Basically, the editor proposed that we simply throw out God's
word and replace it with our individual desires. His editorial
brought these words from St. Augustine to mind:

> It is necessary that we become meek through piety so that we
> do not contradict Divine Scripture, either when it is
> understood and is seen to attack some of our vices, or when it
> is not understood and we feel that we are wiser than it is and

better able to give precepts. But we should rather think and
believe that which is written to be better and more true than
anything which we could think of by ourself, even when it is
obscure.[5]

How different were the attitudes of the Fathers of the
Church, who held God's word in high regard, from the
attitudes that we increasingly encounter today.

Ambiguity Towards God's Word

Even though the direct denial of the authority of God's word
is becoming more and more common, I believe that the indirect
denial of the authority of his word is having an even more
damaging effect. Indirect denial occurs when people ostensibly
honor God's word by saying that we do need to take scripture
into account when making decisions in life, but then add that we
also need to take into account what the latest opinion polls say,
what psychology and sociology tell us, the direction in which
the signs of the times are leading us, and, of course, our own
particular needs in the situation. Such people encourage us to
decide what is right for us on the basis of all these factors.
However, this approach often places God's word on the same
level as majority opinion or theological speculation. Although
such people do not directly repudiate God's word, they relate to
it in such a way that its real authority is drained away and it
becomes one opinion among many—and usually the losing
opinion.

Many people today are undermining God's word by fostering
a certain ambiguity towards it. Preachers, teachers, and counselors, who themselves are uncertain about the authority and
the meaning of God's word, continue to use the words but not to
communicate the conviction or enthusiasm that helps people
know that it is a word they can trust and base their lives on.

This purposeful ambiguity and vagueness about the authority of God's word is even nibbling at the edges of evangelical
gatherings. For example, at the 1982 Convention of Evangelical

Youth Workers in Detroit, a workshop leader, speaking on sex education for junior high school students, recommended that teachers preface their remarks on values with a qualified "in my opinion." Do not give an "overlay" of the Bible, teachers were told; it turns students off. In effect, teachers were discouraged from teaching with authority what God's word says about this area of life. Instead, they should invite sex education experts from public schools and from the county family planning office to educate evangelical youth groups on sexual matters.

Sometimes ambiguity and vagueness are rooted in a fear of being vite considered naive or foolish because of what the next scientific article might reveal. People suspend their commitment to God's word since they no longer envisage it as a clear and certain word. They become addicted to the latest scientific findings in a way that saps their ability to commit themselves definitively to God's word.

Sometimes ambiguity and vagueness is rooted in an actual hostility to the very notion of certainty. In many ways our society has been so deeply affected by the notion of "searching" that the searching becomes an obstacle to finding. The desire not to find can very easily disguise itself as a search.

Silence on God's Word

A third way in which people are undermining God's word is through silence. Preachers, teachers, counselors, and ordinary people experience tremendous pressure from today's society to talk only about those parts of God's word that are least offensive to contemporary culture. In my own church, the Catholic Church, this has meant that for the last fifteen years or so we have heard a lot about God's love but little about his holiness; a lot about how important it is to fulfill ourselves but little about the need to take up the cross and deny ourselves to follow Christ; a lot about what beautiful people we are but little about the need to repent, change, and be conformed to the image of Christ; a lot about how important it is to express our thoughts but little about the need for every thought to be submitted to Jesus Christ. Over a period of years, silence on important aspects of Christian revelation produces a distortion in the life of God's people.

Many passages in scripture starkly and boldly reveal the differences between the divine perspective and the views of our culture. One of them is Matthew 5:29-30: "If your right eye is your trouble, gouge it out and throw it away. Better to lose part of your body than to have it all cast into Gehenna. Again, if your right hand is your trouble, cut it off and throw it away! Better to lose part of your body than to have it all cast into Gehenna." Yet the prevailing spirit of our culture says, "Pay any price you can to be totally whole, even if it means going to Gehenna. Whatever you do, be fulfilled. Whatever you do, protect yourself."

Another passage which flies in the face of the spirit of our age is 1 Corinthians 15:19: "If our hopes in Christ are limited to this life only, we are the most pitiable of men." In spite of what scripture tells us, there is tremendous pressure today to present Christianity only in terms of what it can do for me here and now. But Christianity is not concerned only with what it can do for me today; it is also concerned with the life to come. Christianity is not only about this world; it is also about the world to come.

Note, too, the passage from Matthew 7:13-14: "Enter through the narrow gate. The gate that leads to damnation is wide, the road is clear, and many choose to travel it. But how narrow is the gate that leads to life, how rough the road, and how few there are who find it!" What a different picture this passage presents from the attitude, prevailing in many of our churches, which says that everyone is basically a good person and is going to make it to heaven. The spirit of this age tries to blot out the reality of sin, the truth of God's judgment, the need for redemption, and the fact that you do not simply drift into the kingdom of God; you need to make choices and changes in order to enter his kingdom. As the attitudes of the world work to fog our perception of the divine perspective, the realities of sin, Satan, heaven, hell, judgment, and eternity need to be clearly proclaimed, that the nature and reality of God might be truly revealed.

Reinterpreting Scripture

A fourth way in which people undermine God's word is by reinterpreting it so that it corresponds to causes and desires they are already committed to. Today many people approach God's word with certain preconceptions because they have already made certain ideologies, certain values, into absolutes. This reinterpretation of God's word is expressed in many areas of life. Often it occurs in the realm of politics. Recently a French Catholic priest, who is the secretary of his local section of the Communist party, reinterpreted Christian freedom in this way:

> I fail to see why it would be absurd and contradictory to be both a Christian and a Communist. I will go further: I see no contradiction between being a Marxist and being a man who questions his faith and the ministry he has received from the hands of a bishop. I even dare ask myself and others this question: if Marxist analysis led me to atheism, would this evolution not in fact express the very freedom of the movement of which I am a part? and would this freedom not be the freedom of the Gospel?[6]

Another area where reinterpretation occurs is sexual morality. For example, in one of the workshops at a recent meeting of the Evangelical Women's Caucus, a number of evangelical participants openly defended homosexual practices as compatible with scriptural teaching. (Once again, we see how attacks on God's word are already nibbling at the edges of evangelical groups.)

Another instance of the reinterpretation of scripture in regard to sexual morality comes from a priest who is a moral theologian and who teaches at the main seminary that the Catholic Church maintains in the United States for preparing missionaries. In an article on homosexuality for a national Catholic magazine, he stated:

> But doesn't the Church teach that *active* homosexual persons are sinning? Yes and no. The Church teaches that sex is for having children. This part of the Church's message rings as true as it ever did, and as it always will. The Church also teaches that sex is for loving. It's for loving in marriage, and nowadays, the Church is not so sure that *all* sex-for-love outside marriage is sinful. Surely it is when new life is likely to be generated. People who play around with sex, and then find themselves with unwanted pregnancy, often get abortions. This is the reason the Church opposes sex outside of marriage—family stability for the security of offspring. It's a good reason. Let's hold on to it, you and I who are the Church. But this is not a problem in sex with two people of the same gender. . . . But doesn't the Bible condemn homosexual acts? That it surely does, and roundly. Genesis condemns the men of Sodom and Gomorrah for wishing to have sex with Lot's male guests—by raping them. It is not the homosexuality of mutual respect and self-sacrifice the Scripture condemns here.
>
> But what about Leviticus and the Epistle to the Romans? Do they not call homosexuality an "abomination to the Lord?" Yes, but the outcry is heavily culturally conditioned. . . . Well, we've multiplied and filled the earth, and Jesus the Messiah is already here. Can it be that childless sex is no longer an abomination?[7]

Dozens of articles like this have been published in Catholic publications in recent years, and similar articles are appearing in other Christian publications as well.

Even the area of ecumenism is not immune from reinterpretation of scripture. Unfortunately, we are often confronted with an ecumenical movement that few of us would want to be part of. Two decades ago, for example, the chaplain of an American college wrote a series of articles in which he called for

Christianity to become more relevant to modern man. In the first of these articles, he proposed that "Christianity de-emphasize its claim to uniqueness in favor of a vital universalism, advocating a creative and positive relationship among the religions of the world."[8]

In a second article, he offered the thesis that "the churches should play down their historical, creedal affirmations—the Trinity, number of sacraments, apostolic succession, the deity of Christ, and so on—and work for the abolition of racism, a renewed dedication to human justice and freedom, and greater understanding among the peoples of the world."[9]

Recently he assessed the progress that had been made in the last twenty years in realizing these proposals:

> Almost 20 years later these predictions which raised so much protest seem mild, and most of them have been realized. We've seen a burgeoning of interest in the religions of the East, and even Harvey Cox has belatedly moved in that direction. . . . Except for a phalanx of conservative rearguard figures, I know of no mainstream theologians today, Catholic or Protestant, who are brazen advocates of the uniqueness and once-for-allness of the Christian revelation. . . .[10]

Later in his article, he makes some proposals for the future:

> In the days ahead we should put less emphasis on the historical Jesus. Since Vatican II, Catholics and Protestants have increasingly stressed their agreements. A similar movement is gaining strength between Christians and Jews, as both Catholics and mainstream Protestants are renouncing efforts to evangelize Jews. We are in increasing contact with other religions of the world, and an insistence on the uniqueness of the historical Jesus can only be a hindrance. Christians should never have made a God out of Jesus. It is just too preposterous to believe that God gave his/her world-embracing love uniquely through Jesus. We Christians may use such phrases as "anonymous Christian" and "the cosmic

Christ" in our attempts to universalize Christianity, but then we should empathize with such terms as "the universal Buddha" or "the plurality of avatars. . . ." I suggest that we leave him [Jesus] alone for a while. Just as Jesus said to his disciples, "It's best for you that I depart. For if I do not go, the Advocate will not come to you," so, too, must we have the courage to say that it's best for Jesus to depart for the sake of the love of God.[11]

God forbid that there would be an agreement on such apostasy! The same spiritual force that has tried throughout the ages to destroy our confidence in God's word and in Jesus Christ, the Word of God, is at work today to destroy our confidence once again.

I do not think that we are merely dealing with human weakness, with honest mistakes, or with isolated infidelities. We are dealing with a massive attempt to undermine the authority of God's word for the purpose of destroying God's people here on earth and leading them to eternal damnation. As scripture tells us in 1 Timothy 4:1-2, "The Spirit distinctly says that in latter times, some will turn away from the faith and will heed deceitful spirits and things taught by demons through plausible liars."

The Condition of the World Today

The satanic strategy is one of lies, false teaching, confusion, and undermining the authority of God's word, and it leads to death. A passage from Romans 1:18-31 provides tremendous insight into what is happening in our society today.

The wrath of God is being revealed from heaven against the irreligious and perverse spirit of men who, in this perversity of theirs, hinder the truth. In fact, whatever can be known about God is clear to them; he himself made it so. Since the creation of the world, invisible realities, God's eternal power and divinity, have become visible, recognized through the things he has made. Therefore, these men are inexcusable. They certainly had knowledge of God, yet they did not glorify him as God or give him thanks; they stultified themselves through speculating to no purpose, and their senseless hearts were darkened. They claimed to be wise, but turned into fools instead; they exchanged the glory of the immortal God for images representing mortal man, birds, beasts, and snakes. In consequence, God delivered them in their lusts to unclean practices; they engaged in the mutual degradation of their bodies, these men who exchanged the truth of God for a lie and worshiped the creature rather than the Creator—blessed be he forever, amen! God therefore delivered them up to disgraceful passions. Their women exchanged natural intercourse for unnatural, and the men gave up natural intercourse with women and burned with lust for one another. Men did shameful things with men, and thus received in their own persons the penalty for their perversity. They did not see fit to acknowledge God, so God delivered them up to their own depraved sense to do what is unseemly. They are filled with every kind of wickedness: maliciousness, greed, ill will, envy, murder, bickering, deceit, craftiness. They are gossips and slanderers, they hate God, are insolent, haughty, boastful, ingenious in their wrongdoing and rebellious toward their parents. One sees in them men without conscience, without loyalty, without affection, without pity. They know God's just decree that all who do such things deserve death; yet they not only do them but approve them in others.

One of the characteristics of people who themselves have turned away from God's word is that they encourage other people to do so as well. Misery loves company; there is a superficial brotherhood of the damned.

Today numerous groups are dedicated to leading people away from God's word. And in many ways, the most visible signs of this movement are the sexual confusion and disorder that is becoming more and more prevalent in our society—just as these were the signs that characterized Roman society in St. Paul's time.

We are living in a time of rapid de-Christianization. De-Christianization leads to dehumanization because the only way to be fully human is to be in Jesus Christ. Truly, the wages of sin is death. We are seeing the wages of sin being paid out daily in the environment in which we live, whether it be the 17,000 fetuses that were found in a trash container in California or the spector of nuclear warfare hovering over the entire earth. At a time when the human race is perhaps in the hour of greatest need, God's people are weak, confused, and disunited. This is not accidental; it is part of the satanic plan.

A Time of Visitation

A spiritual war is raging beneath the surface of our society. Yet, in this moment of need, we are also living in a time of tremendous grace and blessing. I believe that we are living in the midst of one of the greatest visitations God has made to his people.

I see many signs of this visitation. First of all, we have the extraordinary ministries of people like Billy Graham, Oral Roberts, and Kathryn Kuhlman, which have touched thousands of people in recent years. We also have some marvellous evangelism ministries, like Campus Crusade, Inter-Varsity, and Navigators, which have touched thousands more. Furthermore, Jesus Christ is being proclaimed to millions through various television ministries.

I think that the Pentecostal movement and charismatic renewal is another sign of this time of visitation. For the first time since the early centuries of Christianity, millions of people are experiencing the signs and wonders of the Holy Spirit in a widespread way.

God is visiting his people for a reason. He is inviting them to turn to him and be saved. He is inviting the church to turn to him and be equipped and empowered because hard times lie ahead. Many people have responded to this visitation, but many more have not. There is a consequence for missing a visitation from God. The consequence is judgment. For this reason, I believe that the destiny of our generation is hanging in the balance.

In Luke 19:41-44, we read about another visitation that God made to his people—the visitation that Jesus made to the people of Jerusalem almost 2,000 years ago:

> Coming within sight of the city, he wept over it and said: "If only you had known the path to peace this day, but you have completely lost it from view! Days will come upon you when your enemies encircle you with a rampart, hem you in, and press you hard from every side. They will wipe you out, you and your children within your walls, and leave not a stone on a stone within you, because you failed to recognize the time of your visitation."

Jesus visited his people—walking through the streets proclaiming the kingdom of God and healing them—but they failed to recognize this moment of grace. A critical moment had arrived; God had sent his only Son. Many responded, but many more did not. Forty years later, the Roman armies destroyed the city of Jerusalem and the Jewish nation was dispersed to the four corners of the earth.

The moment of visitation is a moment of choice. One of the things that determines what happens in this moment of choice is the intercession of God's friends. How much God is willing to do for his friends! Remember the generation of Abraham. When wickedness in Sodom and Gomorrah reached such a point that God had to destroy them, Abraham interceded for the few that were faithful to God, and God saved those few. We see what God was willing to do for his beloved and the weight that he gave to Abraham's prayer.

I believe that the destiny of our generation is hanging right now in the balance. I believe that our generation is faced with a choice: repentance or judgment. We who have been touched by this visitation have a critical role to play. In addition to our evangelistic action, our intercessory prayer is vital in resisting the tide of evil that is flooding our homes and cities.

In conclusion, I would like to offer what I believe to be a particularly important element of our response to the situation in which we find ourselves. It is found in Isaiah 55:6: "Seek the Lord while he may be found, call him while he is near." This, I believe, is the word that the Holy Spirit is bringing to our attention. Now is the time to turn to God. We need to do many important things and to receive a great deal of wisdom. But what we face can only be faced in and with and through the presence of God dwelling with his people. We are not simply dealing with flesh and blood; we are dealing with powers and principalities. Only the power of God, manifesting itself in the words, actions, and lives of his people, is sufficient to face what we are facing. I believe the time has come to repent and turn to God in a more profound way than ever before.

Jesus promised not to leave us orphans. He wants to be with us and guide us. There *is* a way to deal with today's situation, but only God knows this way. We need wisdom from on high. I believe that it is time to turn to God in intercession. The prayers of the friends of God have a tremendous power to change the course of history, to change the fate of our generation.

FOUR

The Loss of a Christian Way of Life

Peter S. Williamson

To this point, the contributors to this volume have concentrated mainly on problems in the faithful teaching of God's word. This essay will address the challenge confronting the people of God not from what they learn in church but from what they learn from the society in which they live. I will focus less on the threat to Christian belief and more on the threat to the way of life the Lord enjoins on his disciples—in particular, some grave and often unrecognized obstacles to passing on our faith to the next generation. I will be speaking mainly about Christians of the industrialized nations of the West and of other nations as they come increasingly to resemble the First World.

"If today someone accused you of being a disciple of Jesus Christ, would there be enough evidence to convict you?" Some of us have heard that question asked in reference to our individual lives; I would like you to consider it in reference to the Christian people. It is a question which focuses our attention not on our beliefs, good intentions, or religious experiences, but on the visible, behavioral consequences of our commitment to Christ. It is a legitimate, biblical test of a believer: "By this it may be seen who are the children of God,

and who are the children of the devil: whoever does not do what
is right is not of God, nor he who does not love his brother"
(1 Jn 3:10) and, "You shall know them by their fruits"
(Mt 7:20).

God's people are to be distinguished from all the other
peoples on earth by practices, customs, and character consistent
with his nature and law. Can those who call themselves
Christians at the close of the twentieth century be recognized by
a way of life that differs from that of the people around them in
its faithfulness to the teaching of Christ? We would have to say
that very many cannot. And today this is not simply the old
problem of many people not quite living up to the Christian
ideal, or some tares among the wheat. Rather there is a process
underway which is erasing the distinguishing behavioral characteristics of Christians.

The fact that some people are revising Christian teaching to
conform to a secular worldview means that the people they
influence will approach ethical decisions in an increasingly
secularized manner. But it is not only teaching that influences
life. There is good reason to say that the opposite is also the
case—that widespread changes in practice among people who
are counted as Christian is giving rise to Christian moral
teaching which is, so to speak, more up to date. The methods of
some accommodating theologians indicates this; for example,
the use of sociological surveys which cite popular practices as an
argument for revising moral norms.

The De-Christianization of Behavior

The picture that emerges from sociological studies in recent
years is one of the persistence of certain key Christian beliefs
but the erosion of Christian behavior. The *Christianity Today*-
Gallup poll in 1980 showed that many people believe the Bible
is God's word, but far fewer read it regularly.[1] Among Roman
Catholics, many experts are of the view that Catholic life is
disappearing into the mainstream of American society. Fr.

Thomas Lynch, director of the Catholic bishops' office on family life, believes that Catholic families in the United States are "more American than they are Catholic. . . . There is an openness to assimilate many of the American values.[2] Fr. Lynch points to the increase of divorce and abortion among Catholics as evidence that Catholics have been abandoning their own values. Another Catholic observer, Fr. Steven Priester, puts it differently. Priester, who directs the Center for the Study of the Family at the Catholic University of America, compares Catholic families to other American families this way: "Their values may differ. But their behavior doesn't."[3]

Christians increasingly bear the stamp of contemporary secular culture in virtually every aspect of life. Here I will comment on four areas: participation in public worship, the handling of material resources, marriage, and chastity.

Most of us are aware of the decrease in church participation in the West during the last few decades, but a quick review is helpful. Many people have simply stopped going to church. Between 1958 and 1982 American church attendance on any given Sunday dropped from 49 to 41 percent of the population. In Canada during the same period, typical Sunday church attendance fell from 53 to 30 percent. Also in the same period, church membership has declined from 73 to 68 percent of the population, continuing a trend since the 1940s.[4] In Europe the situation is far worse, in both the traditionally Protestant countries and the traditionally Catholic ones.

The decline in church attendance and membership is probably the most obvious and familiar indicator of the loss of a Christian way of life. Worship, for an increasing number of people, no longer has any place in life. Even many of those who continue to attend church services do so in a manner which indicates that they are giving low priority to the worship of God.

How people relate to money—the importance they ascribe to its acquisition, how they spend and save it, their ideals regarding material life-style—is an important indicator of their values and the direction of their lives. Christian teaching offers considerable guidance for this aspect of life. It is an area in which the Christian approach and worldly approaches diverge considerably.

Do Christians in the United States today actually deal with their finances and material goods in a distinctive way? Surely some do; but are Christians as a whole distinguishable in this regard from the non-Christians around them? The personal impression that many of us have—that Christians are fairly indistinguishable—received some confirmation in a 1982 study commissioned by the Christian Advertising Forum. That organization was interested in the question from a business point of view—do Christians consititute a recognizable sector of the consumer market that needs special treatment? The pollster concluded his report with these words:

> Do Christians have a different lifestyle from non-Christians? We found surprisingly little evidence of distinction between the two groups on many psychographic indices.... There is a clear distinction between Christianity as a system of beliefs and values, and the manner in which people who profess to be Christians exercise those beliefs and values in their daily lives. The survey results suggest that scriptural exhortations to lead a Christ-like, Bible-based lifestyle are consistently ignored. American Christians have been captivated by secular opportunities and possessions.[5]

The growing instability of Christians' marriages is another aspect of conformity to secular patterns. While some differences have always existed among Protestants, Catholics, and Orthodox regarding the permanence of marriage and the permissibility of divorce, divorce among Christians before the early years of the 20th century was extremely rare. Today it is common, and all segments of the church are affected to some degree. The divorce rate among Roman Catholics in the U.S. is near to (some even say higher than) the national rate.[6] Even the most conservative sectors of American Protantism experience the divorce problem. Jerry Jenkins, former editor of *Moody Monthly,* has named keeping families together one of evangelicals' most serious challenges. Liberal, or mainline, Protestantism has been affected to such a degree that divorce among the laity has been replaced by clergy divorce as the locus of concern. Statistics regarding divorce among Orthodox in the United States are not readily available. However, a Greek Orthodox priest whom I consulted says that divorce among Orthodox is on the increase, though it is less common than in the American population at large. He attributes this difference to the strong family and ethnic ties of Orthodox in America, but predicts that divorce will continue to increase as Orthodox, most of whom have immigrated relatively recently, continue to make their way into the mainstream of American culture.

A somewhat less familiar but equally telling and statistically detectable change in the way of life of Christians in the West is sexual practice among Christian youth. One survey of Protestant churchgoing youths in central Illinois in 1981 found that 59 percent of the males and 42 percent of the females had sexual relations by the age of 18. The unit which conducted the poll was surprised to find no appreciable difference between the sexual behavior of Illinois churchgoing youth and a general population sample of teenagers in California.[7]

Among Catholic youth, a similar situation apparently obtains. Surveys of sexual *behavior* do not seem to have been conducted, but the National Opinion Research Center in Chicago has measured Catholic youths' *attitudes.* (Experts believe there is a high correlation between attitudes and behavior in this area.) The N.O.R.C. survey reflects changes in attitudes over time. Among Catholics in their twenties who receive communion regularly, in 1963 83 percent considered premarital sex wrong; by 1980, only 34 percent considered it wrong.[8] Among all churchgoing youth in the U.S., as of May 1981, 52 percent of youth between the ages of 13 and 18 years did not think premarital sex wrong.[9]

Confronted with data such as this, some people would object

that there have always been Christians who have violated Christian norms for sexual behavior. Is there any reason to think things are worse than in the past?

The answer is that there has in fact been a sexual revolution in Western Europe and the United States since the early 1960s, and that, while there has always been marital infidelity and premarital sex, there has been a dramatic upturn in the incidence of these patterns in the last twenty years. Edward Shorter summarized the evidence on this matter very simply in 1975:

> There are really three things to keep in mind about sex before marriage in the twentieth century: (1) premarital intercourse is now much commoner than in any era since the Middle Ages; (2) although the period 1900-1950 is thoroughly "modern" in comparison with past centuries, little change took place within these years; and (3) the 1960s and early 1970s have witnessed what amounts to a second premarital sexual revolution (the first having occurred at the end of the eighteenth century).

Shorter criticizes those who regard contemporary shifts in adolescent sexual practices as "an optical illusion or an unimportant ripple in the tide of history. Rather, we are now living through a transformation of sexual behavior whose proportions are dramatic and whose implications will long be felt."[10]

The sexual revolution in Western society is one thing; the penetration of the church by this revolution is another, and that is what we are particularly concerned with here. What makes this phenomenon so significant is the key place sexual morality has occupied in the moral teaching of the New Testament and of Christians through the ages. "Know you not that your body is the temple of the Holy Spirit?" Paul inquires. To commit immorality or to persist in it unrepentant is to defile God's temple—the body of the believer and the church. Furthermore, the refusal to adhere to God's law in this respect was regarded, with other violations of the Ten

Commandments, as the kind of wrongdoing which places a person outside the kingdom of God and the church.

> I wrote to you not to associate with any one who bears the name of brother if he is guilty of immorality or greed, or is an idolater, reviler, drunkard, or robber—not even to eat with such a one. (1 Cor 5:11)

> Do you not know that the unrighteous will not inherit the kingdom of God? Do not be deceived; neither the immoral, nor idolaters, nor adulterers, nor homosexuals, nor thieves, nor the greedy, nor drunkards, nor revilers, nor robbers will inherit the kingdom of God. And such were some of you.
> (1 Cor 6:9-11)

The apostolic teaching considers a particular pattern of sexual righteousness to be fundamental to the identity of the Christian people.

The aspects of Christians' lives that we have examined here are more measurable evidences of Christian commitment than many other aspects of behavior. It is easier to determine how many Christian husbands are keeping their solemn vows than how many are loving their wives as Christ loved the church. It easier to determine whether Christians have different patterns of spending money than whether they are growing in forgiveness, love, humility, and truthfulness. Certainly, however, evidence of unfaithfulness to norms which are as clear and objective as Christian teaching on marriage and sexuality suggests that there is not a high level of faithfulness in areas that are harder to define. If half of our churchgoing youth fornicate by the age of 18, what is the likelihood that they will have mastered the finer points of Christian behavior and character?

What about Ascendant Evangelicalism?

During the last several years some highly publicized surveys have suggested that there is a new trend in America that is running opposite to the pattern of de-Christianization. Many of us first heard the news of it in 1976, during the election campaign of Jimmy Carter, with the Gallup report that nearly one-third of all adult Americans had been "born again." Others polls have confirmed these findings and were more specific. Recently, Connecticut Mutual commissioned a poll which found that 49 percent of adult Americans report having had "a specific time in their adult lives in which they made a personal commitment to Christ which changed their lives."[11] In June 1982, the Christian Advertising Forum published very similar results of a poll, cited above, in which 53 percent reported they had "made a personal commitment to Jesus Christ still important in their lives today." The rise of the Moral Majority and the so-called Christian right has also been regarded as a confirmation of this trend.

Some observers have been quick to conclude that a remarkable religious revival is taking place. Some have gone so far as to compare it to the great evangelical awakenings which dramatically shaped the course of British and American history, spawning the abolitionist movement and other social reforms. Some have aleady moved to provide direction for the social and political energies thus released.

I believe this to be a false hope. There is considerable evidence that suggests that Christians are affecting the direction of American culture less and less. Consider the abortion issue, about which most Christians are in basic agreement; or the struggles against pornography or for decent television. In all these instances Christians are battling upstream against the momentum of society. While small gains have been made, the vast energies of our culture are flowing in the opposite direction. Last year Kenneth Kantzer, retiring editor of *Christianity Today,* commented on the influence of evangelicalism on American culture:

My opinion—unprovable, I admit—is that evangelicalism is weaker now than it was 15 years ago, or 50 years ago. People often think it is stronger because they hear more about it in the public media. It certainly has a better press today than it had anytime since the First World War. . . . But the influence of evangelical faith and evangelical ethics on our society is less. As a culture, our nation and, indeed, Western Europe are moving away from biblical Christianity.[12]

Far from being convincing evidence of a national evangelical revival, surveys that uncover large percentages of committed Christians raise the question, where are all these good Christians? In the city where I live I see no indication that nearly half the people around me are personally committed to Jesus Christ. On the contrary, my experience as a leader in a local Christian community is that the members of our community find themselves to be very different in their basic morals and way of life from most of their fellow employees, fellow students, and neighbors. They find relatively few other folks who uphold Christian values in any discernible way, publicly or privately. The surprisingly high percentage of people who claim to be born again and the meager evidence of effects on individuals and society speak eloquently against the notion that we are dealing with a great religious awakening. I believe the data point to another interpretation, namely, that widespread expressions of Christian belief or commitment do not say anything about whether those people are living as Christians. It suggests, further, that de-Christianization is present in two forms: those who drop out of church and consciously relinquish their Christian beliefs, and those who retain what they consider to be a personal commitment to Christ, and perhaps even attend church, but whose lives in other respects are completely unaffected.

The idea that church members are being de-Christianized in a manner which for the time being does not cause them to drop out but instead to accommodate gains credence from our daily experience of what is taking place among Christians. It has become normal for Christianized versions of virtually every secular trend to appear, whether it be in music, counseling approaches, family life self-help books, survivalism, sex manuals, money management techniques, social or political causes, both on the right and on the left. Many of these books, movements, and fashions carry a Christian label, but the content, toned down perhaps and tailored slightly to please a different clientele, is fundamentally unchanged. Let me hasten to say that I see great value in taking helpful secular knowledge or cultural forms and making them genuinely Christian, and some Christians are doing precisely that. But more than words and water are required for efficacious baptism; faith and conversion must also be present. It is my perception that many people have lost their Christian moorings and are drifting with whatever wind is strongest.

The evidence for a loss of a distinct Christian way of life among Christians should move church leaders to consider as candidates for evangelism not only the unchurched and those who have dropped out, but also those who attend church and profess a commitment to Christ. Certainly the washout of Christian distinctives in behavior is not equally true everywhere in the churches, and perhaps there are some parts of the Christian West which have hardly experienced these changes at all. What should concern us all is that there is a *trend* here; this is the *direction* things are going in. It is of the utmost importance that Christian leaders understand the processes that are at work. It will not do to trust in past successes, or in the numerical or financial strength of our churches and Christian institutions. Nor should we succumb to the temptation to comfort ourselves because our particular corner of the Lord's vineyard has so far escaped the blight or is not as affected as our neighbor's plot.

The Processes

The social changes which have led to Christians' loss of a distinct way of life have been analyzed by historians and sociologists such as Jacques Ellul, Peter Berger, Marion Levy, Jr., and Robert Nisbet. They do not all approach the subject with Christian concerns, but their analyses imply conclusions for Christians. (The introduction of this book offers an overview.) I want to underscore the importance of two major trends that are contributing to the de-Christianization of the churches, particularly of the daily lives of their members.

The first is the de-Christianization of Western society, with its accompanying hostility to Christian beliefs and behavior. This change in orientation has been occurring since the Enlightenment, but has accelerated since the First World War. It is apparent under a variety of forms. The encroachment of the ideology of secular humanism on almost every aspect of culture is an obvious example; so is the penetration of other secular ideologies, such as Marxism and radical feminism. The sexual revolution constitutes a major turning of society away from Christian mores. Influential schools of psychology—Freudian, Jungian, Skinnerian, and selfist—while they teach much that is true and helpful, present interpretations of man, his needs, and the solutions to his problems which are, at root, opposed to Christian revelation. Last, but by no means least, pervasive materialism and affluence have produced a soil that is not hospitable to the gospel seed.

In the past, Catholics and Protestants in the West and Orthodox in the East relied on society at large to share their basic moral values and reinforce them by law, custom, and popular opinion. It was not so necessary to teach Christians a way of life distinct from that of the surrounding society, not only because most of the people were also Christians of one kind or another but because even those who were not Christians subscribed to similar standards of truthfulness, justice, faithfulness in marriage, responsibility, honor, self-control, and so on. That broad consensus no longer exists. Not only can law and popular morality no longer be relied on to reinforce Christian values; "anti-moral moralities" exist and are even written into law. A prime example is the legal sanction of a mother taking the life of her unborn child, based on high-sounding notions of individual rights and concern for quality of life.

It might be hoped that this trend could at least be held at bay where Christianity is fervently believed and practiced; and indeed, to some degree, it has been. But a second trend makes it very difficult for Christians to maintain their distinctiveness: a process that may be summarized as the breakdown of natural community.

When people live together and have a substantial commitment to one another—whether it is within the nuclear family or in larger groupings such as a village, an ethnic neighborhood, a rural parish, a kinship group or tribe—they live according to a common way of life, and pass it on to newcomers and to the next generation. Their relationships with one another enable them, to varying degrees, to maintain a set of beliefs, values, and customs distinct from the surrounding society. In the past, and to some extent in the present, Christians have lived in stable, committed relationships that have helped them preserve a Christian way of life. Actually, these have always been particular—an immigrant Polish Catholic, German Lutheran, Greek Orthodox, Dutch Reformed, or Southern Baptist way of life, or simply the way of life of the Fentons, the Wagners, or the McCoys.

But today, social historians tell us, the groups intermediate between the individual and society at large are dissolving, losing their cohesiveness and influence on their members, leaving individuals much more susceptible to the influence of whatever beliefs, values, and customs are prevalent in the larger society. It becomes more difficult for any group within society to maintain its own ways and to hand them on to the next generation.

The reasons for this development are complex. Urbanization, the collectivization of labor, and a high degree of personal mobility undermine stable community life, as does the diversity of opportunities that modern life presents. Furthermore, popular ideals of individual fulfillment and personal autonomy over against the traditional claims of the smaller community have a centrifugal effect. For these reasons and others, modern society tends toward a mass society of individuals detached from subgroupings that would link them together by mutual commitment in a distinct way of life.

One might assume that a mass society of autonomous individuals would be a free society marked by diverse ways of living, but in fact there is a strong contrary tendency. Though there may be a sense of personal freedom and a certain amount of deviation from social norms, without strong intermediate groups the tendency is for individuals to become more and more conformed to prevailing social patterns. The precondition for a truly pluralistic society is the presence of discrete intermediate groups which help individuals live a distinct way of live. The breakdown of natural community in ethnic groups, parishes and congregations, neighborhoods and towns, and the family itself tends to homogenize the members of society, making them subject to whatever voices, rhythms, and patterns are strongest in the environment. For Christians at the end of the twentieth century, this is not good news. (The effects of the breakdown of mediating social groupings are explored in various ways by Ellul in *Propaganda* and Nisbet in *The Quest for Community*.)

Media, Experts, and the World of Youth

The mass culture is communicated to individuals in many ways. I will touch briefly on three very important change agents. First are the mass media. No generation before ours has spent so much of its time being entertained, educated, and formed by television, radio, movies, newspapers, and magazines, and so little time being taught a way of life by their families and the Christian communities they belong to. The media provide a common set of experiences and a powerful worldview to millions who are offered the same selection of information and opinions, and the modeling of the same particular beliefs, values, and priorities.

Second is the plethora of secular experts, mostly from the social sciences, who professionally and popularly explain how to cope with life, how to raise your children, how to facilitate your children's moral development, how to be happily married, how to handle your money, how to grow old, and so on. These secular experts provide a constant stream of instruction in what to believe and how to live. For Christians, they constitute a rival teaching authority.

One should not underestimate the impact of social changes—proposed by secular experts and amplified and reiterated by the media—on adults whose attitudes and values one might assume were more or less fixed. For example, it is my observation that many middle-class American Catholics and Protestants between the ages of 50 and 60, who grew up in a very different climate than prevails today, have substantially altered their views about important family issues such as sex roles and parental discipline, and their attitudes toward moral issues such as adultery, homosexual behavior, and divorce. For many this change has been so gradual that they have not noticed how considerably they have changed.

Third, public education dominates the lives of our society's children between the ages of six and eighteen (preschool and college lengthen the period at both ends). Besides educating children in the three R's, the educational system communicates a great deal about life. Recently the secular worldview and values of public education have attracted a great deal of scrutiny from Christians. But of even greater significance than the content of public education is the socializing effect of the peer environments it creates. It is the disjuncture of this youthful peer environment and the parents' generation that I want to examine more closely.

It has become normal for children past the primary school level to identify with and seek the approval primarily of those who are their own age or slightly older. A separation between the generations results and frustrates from the outset any serious effort to pass on a way of life from parents to children. Increasingly, the children "decide for themselves" under the potent influence of the peer group and the role models of the media. To the extent that the formation of children's lives takes place under adult supervision, it takes place under the auspices of public servants who may share few of the parents' beliefs and values. Under this arrangement any effort to pass on a faith and a way of life from one generation to another is doomed. Occasionally, and to a limited degree, strengthening the nuclear family enables parents to transmit the Christian way of life and set of values to their children—but less often than we like to admit. This leads to a key insight about how the process of de-Christianization takes place. The greatest change does not occur in the life of individual adults during their lifetimes; it occurs between generations.

Most of us who read this are sufficiently old that, whether we like to acknowledge it or not, our orientation to life is fairly well set. Our beliefs and behavior can change, but our fundamental outlook is established. Perhaps one could express it crudely by saying that by the age of 25 an individual has 75 percent of his or her approach to life fixed. Barring some dramatic experience such as divorce or religious conversion, the person will probably alter his approach to life only to a moderate degree, no matter how much television he watches or how many books he reads. The major formative period for the settling of a person's basic convictions is the period between 15 and 25 years of age. My fifteen years' experience in working with university students would indicate that the last two years of secondary school and the first two of college are the key years for most young people.

During most of this ten-year period, modern youth are highly influenced by their peer group and those a few years older. Remarkably little real communication and influence passes from parents to children or from older adults to young adults in this age range. With their peers young people share a set of life circumstances, problems, choices, and opportunities that are very different from those their parents face. They dress differently and have their own music—which their parents usually want no part of. I do not think it is an exaggeration to say that parents and their children during this 10-year period are thought-worlds apart, the parents having little or no idea what really motivates their children, or what takes place when their children and their friends gather. The problem is particularly acute between parents who are Christians and their children who have grown up in a secular mileau, and it is particularly manifest in the parents' ignorance of what is taking place in regard to sex or drinking or drugs.

Not only are there important differences between generations, but also between successive waves, or "age cohorts," of children and young adults within a generation. The style and tone of the youth culture of 17-year-olds today, for example, is different from that of 17-year-olds in 1975. The youth environment is constantly changing. New fashions in music and clothing are constantly surfacing. How different were the experiences and perspectives of college students of the fifties, sixties, and seventies from one another! Though the most apparent and colorful traits of differentiation disappear when styles change and students are absorbed into the work force, the fact remains that the young people grew up and evolved much of their approach to life at significantly different cultural moments.

The significance of these successive waves of change is that a much wider difference opens between parents and children, who are two or three "minigenerations" apart. The pace of cultural change from one generation to another has thus picked up. Given the rapidity of change, within a generation of twenty-five to thirty years, a drastic departure from the beliefs and way of life of the preceding generation results. My impression is that through both the seemingly radical and conservative pendulum swings of the American youth culture during the last couple decades, that culture has grown consistently and swiftly less consistent with the Christian way of life. This is a change which I believe people who have not had the opportunity to be close to it have not adequately perceived. While some Christian youth environments have resisted the extremes of the secular mass youth culture, Christian young people, on the whole, have followed the same patterns and have been formed in similar attitudes.

If we think of the loss of a Christian way of life not primarily in terms of ourselves but in terms of our children, clearly the issue is, can we pass on Christian beliefs and a Christian way of life to our children? Granted, this is never something that can be done simply by the parents; each individual child must make a personal choice for Christ and his ways. Nevertheless, Christians throughout the ages have counted on being able to transmit their faith to the next generation.

But, in fact, this is where I see the greatest loss taking place among those who are committed Christians. Many, I could even say most, of the children of committed Christians whom I know, do not go on to share their parents' convictions and way of life. The children do not usually end up evil or hostile towards their parents' committed Christian life-style. It is simply "not for them." They do not mind their parents' Christian convictions so long as they are not pushed to come along. In cases where the children do go on to live as committed Christians, it is usually because something later in life converts them. It is not that their parents and church successfully passed Christianity on to them. The best that most Christian parents today can give their children is pre-evangelism—the example of a good life and the understanding that this is related to their Christian beliefs.

A Spiritual Struggle

This process of de-Christianization has penetrated different parts of the Western world, different towns, different churches, different families to varying degrees. The rate of attrition is not nearly so bad in many places as I have described—I live in the highly de-Christianized environments of Ann Arbor and the University of Michigan. Nevertheless, the change is widespread, and Christians who live in more protected and peaceful regions should heed the words of those stationed on the frontiers.

Most of us recognize the problem that occurs when Christians no longer believe the fundamental truths of the Christian message. That is the most obvious fruit of de-Christianization, and the one we find easiest to respond to. It is also true that there is so much to be done simply to respond to this problem that we can be kept busy and fail to appreciate how grave is the problem of the loss of a Christian way of life. This would be a mistake, partly because if we lose a Christian way of life we are likely to lose our beliefs as well. But we recognize it as an even more serious mistake when we understand the absolute inadequacy, from God's point of view, of a faith that does not issue in holy living. Scripture makes it clear that our redemption is intended to result in a changed way of life:

> For the grace of God has appeared for the salvation of all men, training us to renounce irreligion and worldly passions, and to live sober, upright, and godly lives in this world, awaiting our blessed hope, the appearing of the glory of our great God and Savior Jesus Christ, who gave himself for us to redeem us from all iniquity and to purify for himself a people of his own who are zealous for good deeds. (Ti 2:11-14)

Scripture uses the word "holy" to describe the kind of life that God desires his people to lead: "As obedient children, do not be conformed to the passions of your former ignorance, but as he who called you is holy, be holy yourselves in all your conduct; since it is written, 'You shall be holy, for I am holy'" (1 Pt 1:14-16). In the Old Testament passage that Peter is quoting, the Lord was concerned precisely with the necessity of his people *not* living in the manner of the surrounding peoples but instead sharing in his own character:

> You shall therefore keep all my statutes and all my ordinances, and do them; that the land where I am bringing you to dwell may not vomit you out. And you shall not walk in the customs of the nation which I am casting out before you; for they did all these things, and therefore I abhorred them. But I have said to you, "You shall inherit their land, and I will give it to you to possess, a land flowing with milk and honey." I am the Lord your God, who have separated you from the peoples. . . . You shall be holy to me; for I the

Lord am holy, and have separated you from the peoples, that you should be mine. (Lv 20:22-24, 26)

If holiness in behavior was an essential requirement under the Old Covenant, how much more must it characterize us who have the Holy Spirit and God's law written not on tablets of stone but on our hearts? The words of Jesus to his disciples reveal how important for the whole earth is the distinctness and faithfulness of Christians, and warn us of the consequences of failing: "You are the salt of the earth; but if salt has lost its taste, how shall its saltness be restored? It is no longer good for anything except to be thrown out and trodden under foot by men" (Mt 5:13).

This, then, is the problem of the church of the West. We are losing a distinctly Christian way of life and are coming more and more to resemble the non-Christian societies around us. Even when our beliefs remain the same, the world is forming us. The salt of the earth is losing its savor. More and more Christians of the West have the reputation of being alive, but in fact are dead. Is the time coming when Christ will take away our lampstand? Surely we Christians of the West will not escape judgment. Those among us to whom a stewardship has been entrusted should prepare to give an account. Surely all of us are being summoned to faithfulness ourselves and to do all we can to strengthen our brothers and sisters.

How do we respond now to the twin problems of rejection of Christian teaching and the loss of a Christian way of life among those bearing the name of Christian? Certainly a pastoral response is called for—a strategy that will help Christians remain faithful to the Lord and his teaching in the unique conditions of modern life. We must discover a way for Christians to live as distinct communities of one kind or another and so avoid disappearing into secularized mass society. We must overcome the considerable difficulties and learn how to pass on our faith and way of life to our children.

But we would be nearsighted indeed if we only perceived the

problem of the loss of a Christian way of life *sociologically*, or even as a strictly pastoral problem. Behind the sociological phenomenon there is spiritual warfare, an attack on the Lord's people that must be repelled. "Our battle is not against human forces but against the principalities and powers, the rulers of this world of darkness, the evil spirits in regions above" (Eph 6:12). Our "adversary the devil prowls around like a roaring lion, seeking someone to devour" (1 Pt 5:8). We must resist him, firm in our faith, individually and corporately, with the spiritual weapons given us—prayer and the word of God. We must put on God's own armor of righteousness, truth, the hope of salvation, and the gospel of peace. And having done all this, we must stand firm.

But we should not look exclusively outside ourselves for the roots of the problem. When God's enemies are getting the best of God's people, it often indicates that something is not right with God's people. Psalm 81:8-16 reveals God's attitude and the first response we must make:

Hear, O my people, while I admonish you!
    O Israel, if you would but listen to me!
There shall be no strange god among you;
    you shall not bow down to a foreign god.
I am the Lord your God,
    who brought you up out of the land of Egypt.
    Open your mouth wide, and I will fill it.

"But my people did not listen to my voice;
    Israel would have none of me.
So I gave them over to their stubborn hearts,
    to follow their own counsels.
O that my people would listen to me,
    that Israel would walk in my ways!
I would soon subdue their enemies,
    and turn my hand against their foes.
Those who hate the Lord would cringe toward him,
    and their fate would last for ever.

I would feed you with the finest of the wheat,
and with honey from the rock I would satisfy you."

We must listen to God's voice and rely on his counsel. We must repent and return to God's ways. We must implore his help. Then we will see his salvation.

FIVE

Orthodox, Protestants, Roman Catholics: What Basis for Cooperation?

Stephen B. Clark

I WOULD NOT BE SURPRISED if, during the course of this conference, each of us has wondered, "Why are we all here together? What can people of our diversity do together that would not be a waste of time?" Yet we do find many common concerns and much similarity in the ways we view things, even when we come from what in the past would have been regarded as widely differing theological positions. I personally do not believe, however, that similar concerns and views form an adequate basis for cooperation. Therefore I want to give two other reasons for cooperation.

The first is simply common need. Christians who maintain historic Christian beliefs in the world today need help. It is unclear whether we need help just to survive. But we need help badly enough that we cannot spurn help as a luxury. And often the cause of Christ is suffering because we do not come together and help one another.

For example, the community to which I belong has found itself in regular outreach to Malaysia. We have received many visitors and a variety of requests for help. For several years now, Malaysia's Mohammedan government has been persecuting Christians. The persecution is not violent, but it is constant and increasing, and is partly executed by legislation that restricts the ability of the Christians to function. Besides the normal anti-missionary legislation, Malaysia has legislation which restrains native Christians from carrying out standard church functions, and more restrictions seem to be on the way. In addition, the government is pouring large sums of money into converting Christians to Mohammedanism. Not only does it hire Mohammedan proselytizers and finance the production of a great deal of propaganda, it also uses the schools, including Christian schools, to indoctrinate Christian children. Yet when I visited Malaysia, I was amazed to find that in this situation, there is almost no cooperation between Catholics and Protestants. Surely in a situation like this, we could see the value of cooperation. We might also see the effect in Malaysia of the decreasing cooperation among Christians around the world. Many people are remarking these days upon the success of the solidarity of American Jews with Israel's ability to maintain itself in the world today. The situation of the Christians in Malaysia is a testimony to the opposite—the low solidarity of Christians with one another internationally.

Let me take a different example closer to home. I have been impressed by the recent efforts among conservative evangelical Christians to start Christian schools in the United States. I have also been struck by how many of them would appreciate getting some of the tax money that parents pay for education to go to their own schools and not just to public schools. I have been struck even more with how many of their arguments are the same I heard Catholics using when I first became aware of the issues twenty years ago. Now, however, they are coming from the same sort of people who tended to be among the most vigorous opponents of parochial education in the '50s. I cannot help wondering whether, if we had been able to get a strong coalition of Catholics and evangelicals working together in the '50s, all Christians might now have more money available for their schools and the survival of their children's Christianity—and morality.

These are contemporary examples. History provides many more. Many historians, with good grounds, attribute the beginning of the de-Christianization of Western Europe to the wars between the Catholics and Protestants in the 16th and 17th centuries. That certainly is a heavy price to pay for hostility. Perhaps the most striking example of Christians' failure to achieve cooperation is the Fourth Crusade. While it is too much to attribute the Fourth Crusade completely to religious disunity, religious enmity did play a part. As a result, Western crusaders destroyed the power of the Christian Byzantine empire, the one force which had been a bulwark against Turkish invasion, and within a hundred years or so of that crusade, the Crusaders' descendants began to see the Turks conquer Catholic as well as Orthodox countries and begin a rule of oppression and religious persecution that lasted for centuries. One is reminded of the teaching of 2 Chronicles 28.

The lessons are not all bitter ones, though. We see positive results of cooperation among Christians, too. The battle in this country against abortion has certainly gained a great deal of strength from the cooperation between Catholics and evangelicals, a cooperation that might even be on the increase. Inspiring examples are often given to us from Christians suffering violent persecutions in many countries of the world today. I recently read a statement in *Christianity Today* by an evangelical leader in Czechoslovakia who said, "Suffering has shown us that we can survive without church structures. But we cannot survive without other Christians. Many of us learned that lesson in prison cells when we suffered together with Orthodox and Catholic believers. We discovered that [what mattered was] our central commitment to Jesus Christ."[1]

Common Theological Challenges

Some have predicted that it will only be common external enemies that will drive Christians together into unity. That may be the case, but there are other grounds of common need besides external enemies. We also have common challenges. For most of us, the chief challenge at the moment is the presence of what we have called theological liberals, modernists, or theological secularists within the churches to which we belong. An understanding of their appearance in the churches, and of the background of their thinking, indicates that in our different theological traditions we are encountering a common problem, although it takes somewhat different forms in various churches.

To describe the phenomenon, I prefer the term "theological secularism."* "Theological secularism" is the descendant of nineteenth-century Protestant liberalism. It began with a desire on the part of many Christians to accommodate themselves to the then dominant ideology, classical liberalism, the result of Enlightenment thinking. Liberalism was hostile to doctrine or dogma—truths held on authority, and held with the conviction of certainty and not simply as tentative hypotheses. It was likewise hostile to moral constraints imposed on human beings from outside authority, either the authority of tradition or the authority of revelation. Because of this, in fact, it tended to be unfriendly to community—although the classical liberals would never have said such a thing—because community depends on corporate norms that come to an individual from outside himself and, if it lasts very long, on tradition.

In nineteenth-century Protestant churches, most notably in Germany, many Christians attempted to combine liberalism with Christianity. They adopted many of the characteristic liberal positions, and they also adopted many of the liberal

---

*I prefer to use the term "theological secularist" rather than "liberal," as some do, because a broader term is more accurate and also because of the great number of meanings of the word "liberal." It can, for instance, frequently mean simply the antithesis of "conservative" and signify those who are willing to make changes. For instance, many of those in the Catholic Church today who would be wholeheartedly behind Pope John Paul II in his attack on the theological secularists would not wish to back his conservative approach to Catholic life in the same way, and hence might validly be described as liberal.

critiques of traditional Christianity. The result was a denial of the paramount authority of scripture and of church doctrinal formulations, and a reinterpretation of Christian doctrines, such as the atonement, to mean something acceptable to the society around them. A Christianity with a severely reduced content remained, which coexisted rather peacefully with the surrounding culture. The Protestant liberals by no means intended to attack Christianity—they thought, in fact, that they were helping it. Instead, they had an undermining effect on it, sapped its vitality, and paved the way for a loss of membership.

As Protestant liberalism has developed it has, in recent years, extended its influence into the Roman Catholic Church. It has also given rise to other streams which could not be described as liberalism in the old sense. Some are Marxist. Some are "Hindu indigenist." It would hardly do, for instance, to describe certain modern Catholic liberation theologians as Protestant liberals, but they do have some very important characteristics in common with them, and their ancestry can be traced back to them. It is from the Protestant liberals that they learned how to approach Christianity as if it were a religion that did not base itself on a supernatural God intervening in human history and speaking to men, establishing beliefs and practices with his authority. And it was from the Protestant liberals that the Catholic liberation theologians learned how to reinterpret the meaning of central Christian doctrines so that these doctrines coincided in meaning with the key tenets of non-Christian ideologies, in this case, the Marxist ideology. They learned from the Protestant liberals, in other words, the reductionism that Peter Berger, in "Secular Theology and the Rejection of the Supernatural," defined as a procedure in which "the contents of the religious tradition, with which the theologian continues to identify in some manner, are translated *in full* into language that (or so it is intended) will no longer be in cognitive dissonance with the secularized milieu."[2] Those we can call theological secularists belong to this broader movement within the Christian churches today, which includes not only Protes-

tant liberals but also Marxists and the adherents of other
ideologies attractive to those who would still like to identify
with Christianity.

Over the years, Catholics, evangelicals, and also Orthodox
have responded to theological secularism in similar ways.
However, few realize just how similar were the original
Fundamentalist movement and the antimodernist campaign
under Pius X, and on how much they agreed. A good book of
comparison still waits to be written.

Today, theological secularism is a common problem for both
Catholics and evangelicals, the very groups that resisted it so
strongly seventy-five years ago. It has been on the rise since the
'60s, when it began to affect Roman Catholics in a significant
way. In the '70s it began to invade the evangelical world. My
observation is that it is not without influence among Eastern
Orthodox and Oriental Orthodox as well. This conference has
addressed the erosion of theological secularism and other
currents that sap the strength of Christianity, and we have
seen how the lessons in one church are often applicable to
another. We could learn from one another's experience and
wisdom, and it would be promising for us to cooperate in this
area.

Brothers and Sisters in Christ

There are, then, many practical reasons for cooperation that
come out of our common need to survive and serve as Christians
in a difficult environment. But there is another reason which I
personally find more compelling—the theological fact of our
brotherhood and sisterhood in Christ. If we are brothers and
sisters in Christ, we ought to be able to love one another. That
does not just mean that we should feel sentiments of solidarity
during the week of prayer for Christian unity. It means that we
should be committed to one another in an ongoing, practical
way.

I would like to turn to a teaching in scripture that does not get
the attention that it deserves. The teaching is expressed most

clearly in the First Letter of John, although it is to be found in many other places in scripture. As you know, 1 John is concerned with distinguishing between "those who have gone out from us," a group that many would identify as a Gnostic or proto-Gnostic sect, and true Christians. John picks out a number of marks of true Christians: belief in what we would now call the doctrine of the Incarnation, a moral Christian life, and the experience of the Spirit. In addition, he picks out love of the brethren as an identifying mark essential to being a Christian.

By "the brethren" or "brothers and sisters" John means fellow Christians. In this he follows the usage of the rest of the New Testament, except where the term is used to mean "fellow elders," and, of course, where it means natural brothers and sisters. The New Testament, scholarship tells us, never speaks of the brotherhood of the human race. That does not mean that the idea of some solidarity with the human race is foreign to Christian revelation. It simply means that we cannot read such a notion into places where the word "brethren" is used in the New Testament. "Brethren" or "brothers and sisters" means "fellow Christians," and "love of the brethren," as the phrase in 1 John is rendered in the Revised Standard Version, means "love of our fellow Christians."

First John stresses the love of the brethren in several places. Chapter 3:13-18 summarizes the teaching well and states it in a way we cannot easily ignore: "We know that we have passed out of death into life, because we love the brethren. He who does not love remains in death. . . . By this we know love, that he laid down his life for us and we ought to lay down our lives for the brethren. But if any one has the world's goods and sees his brother in need, yet closes his heart against him, how does God's love abide in him? Little children, let us not love in word or speech, but in deed and in truth." This, and similar passages, have often been used in merely humanitarian ways, but while there may be humanitarian passages in scripture, this is not one of them. It is very evangelical. In attempting to state the marks by which to distinguish true Christians from false brethren,

John is interested in criteria which directly relate to the fundamental reality at the core of Christianity—our relationship to Christ himself and to his work of redemption. He chooses love of fellow Christians, since to love fellow Christians *because* they are Christians is to recognize the importance of belonging to Christ. As the gospel saying puts it, the relationship we have with fellow disciples is more important than the relationship with our mother and natural brothers and sisters. Love of the brethren is an external, behavioral indication of a genuinely Christian spiritual state.

First John says some strong things about the love of the brethren. It says that it is essential. It says, in fact, that if we do not love the brethren, we do not have eternal life in us. On that basis, 1 John sees it as obligatory. We are obligated to lay down our lives for our brothers and sisters in Christ, and laying down our lives at least involves the sharing of goods with them when they are in need. We have, in short, concrete duties toward them, duties which touch our pocketbooks. Further study of the scriptural teachings on love of the brethren would indicate that we have considerably more obligations towards them, such as defending them when enemies attack them, and so on. In other words, scripture teaches that we do have special obligations to our fellow Christians, and fulfilling them is essential to being a Christian.

Such a statement leads naturally to the question, "Who, then, is my brother in Christ?" Tackling that question theologically would detain us in an issue of sufficient size to keep us from discussing anything else here. Rather than doing that, I simply want to observe that in the course of the last fifty to seventy-five years, there has been a massive change in attitude among the Christian people. The result of that change is that we here at this conference are likely a body of Christians who all recognize one another as Christians, even though we represent a considerable diversity of theological conviction and church loyalty.

Many of us might want to add some qualification to the term "brother," such as "separated brother." Most of us would not go on to recognize all the churches that others belong to as fully acceptable as churches or perhaps even as churches at all. I would not be surprised if some of us were still of the opinion that the Catholic Church is an apostate church, and the Roman Catholic Church has not yet officially come to the point of recognizing Protestant bodies as anything more than "ecclesial communities." Nonetheless, that does not obscure the significance of the revolution I am describing. A hundred years ago, Roman Catholics would have normally viewed Protestants as people who needed conversion to Christianity and who would only be saved by way of exception when they had a desire for the truth but because of ignorance could not recognize it in the Catholic Church. And, many, if not most, Protestants would have returned the compliment. Many Protestants still view Catholics and Orthodox in such a way. But a large number of Catholics, Orthodox, and evangelicals are at the point of recognizing one another as Christians, Christians who have made some serious theological errors and who belong to faulty churches, no doubt, but Christians nonetheless. They would not extend that recognition to all of the members of the other groups, and there is certainly no way of getting us all to agree on where to draw the line, but we do take the perspective that a large number of members of all the other churches turn out to be Christians. That, then, puts us in the place of needing to recognize a gospel demand for cooperation that goes beyond the Christians in our own church to whomever we can see to be true Christians, and that recognition will at least unite a substantial number of evangelicals, Catholics, and Orthodox.

Second Chronicles 28:1-15 provides a scriptural illustration of the importance of this obligation. It narrates a war between Israel and Judah, fought under Ahaz of Judah and Pekah of Israel. Israel resoundingly defeats Judah and leads many of them into captivity to slavery. As they are bringing the captives back, the prophet Obed goes out to meet the returning troops with this message:

> Behold, because the Lord, the God of your fathers, was angry with Judah, he gave them into your hand, but you have slain

them in a rage which has reached up to heaven. And now you intend to subjugate the people of Judah and Jerusalem, male and female, as your slaves. Have you not sins of your own against the Lord your God? Now hear me, and send back the captives from your brethren whom you have taken, for the fierce wrath of the Lord is upon you. (2 Chr 28:9-11)

We should note a few things here. First, Israel and Judah were in a state of schism and had no united government. Nor was either in a fully acceptable spiritual position from the other's point of view—or from God's. Second, God did not rebuke them for fighting one another. He seemed to regard some fighting between them as acceptable and even seemed to view it as a punishment of Judah's sins. But he was very concerned that they had not followed the rules of how to treat brothers during their conflict. The Israelites slaughtered their defeated brothers and led them back captive to enslave them. They also, as the next verses make clear, neglected to provide for their needs: food, clothing, shelter, and medical care. I might note here that many of us fail to perceive the significance of this passage because we have lost an awareness of the view that there are different rules of fighting that apply depending on the relationship, a view that was certainly accepted in the Old Testament. The chief point is simply that even in such an unlikely situation as that in 2 Chronicles 28, the Lord was very angry when his people did not treat their brethren as brethren.

What sort of brotherly love might be practical and appropriate in a group like ours? One area would be cooperation in missionary and evangelistic work. I have been impressed with much of the missionary study and writing that emerges from places like the Fuller School of World Mission and the U.S. Center for World Mission. I have noted how often their writings draw lessons from Catholic missionary workers. Yet I rarely see indications that Catholics are aware of them.

I can add a personal observation. As you know, the community to which I belong, The Word of God, is what we call an ecumenical community, that is, a community composed of

Christians from differing church backgrounds. We did not start out being ecumenical, though. And we did not originally decide to be an ecumenical community primarily because we wanted to be ecumenical. In fact, two of the first leaders of our community were rebuked by a Catholic bishop the year before our community began for not being adequately cooperative with the Catholic Church's new ecumenical interests. Some of the original Protestant leaders of our community have testified that they came to our group, before it was much of a community, because they thought it might provide a chance for them to save some Catholics. We started being ecumenical because of the new openness in the '60s that drew together Christians of a wide variety of churches into grassroots renewal movements and local groups. Many of those groups, however, either faded, affiliated with a church body, or became churches themselves. We were one of the groups that remained ecumenical and I believe a key reason was that we began a serious effort at evangelism.

As we evangelized together, we discovered that we were more effective than we would have been if we had evangelized along denominational lines. Modern Americans are not nearly as responsive to Catholic evangelism or Orthodox evangelism or Lutheran evangelism as they are to basic Christian evangelism. Many people do not discover this, because what they describe as evangelism is either a form of church renewal or a form of retrieving ex-church members. They either appeal to people in church environments or those who once were affiliated with a church environment. However, when we go to evangelize in a secular environment such as a student or business environment, and appeal to all the people in the environment, then we discover the limitations of denominational evangelism.

As our community became more successful in evangelism, we found ourselves a growing body of people who had come to a deeper Christian commitment, but who did not want to leave our churches. That has been a constant complication of our community life, one that in many ways we might have preferred to avoid, but one that has unexpectedly put us in positions where we found we could do the Lord's work where others were not able to. The chief benefit, however, that it has provided for us locally has been the ability to evangelize effectively.

Another area in which Christians could cooperate is spiritual renewal. We can be helpful to one another in learning how to be more effective in spiritual renewal. The Catholic charismatic renewal is a movement in the Roman Catholic Church that has clearly gained some of its effectiveness in spiritual renewal from lessons it learned from evangelicals. Catholic charismatics were initially criticized for bringing Protestant revivalism into the Catholic Church. (The attacks normally centered more on questions of culture and technique than on doctrinal matters.) However, when one traces the history of revivalism back to its roots in the 17th and 18th centuries, one finds that the Protestant renewal movements had learned from earlier Catholic "revivalists," especially the friars. Accounts of medieval Catholic revivalism such as "The Great Alleluia" of 1234 would no doubt curl the hair of some of the modern Catholic critics. At any rate, the history of renewal movements shows an ecumenical sharing that has been both successful and helpful.

Yet another area for making our brotherly love practical is the sharing of pastoral wisdom. We clearly confront the same challenges, because we live in the same society. Normally, the same things work or don't work when employed by Protestants, Catholics, or Orthodox. Here I would give *Pastoral Renewal* magazine as a good example of how we find many of the same things helpful.

Cooperative Ecumenism

I have pointed out two important bases for cooperation. Now I would like to discuss an obstacle that we need to deal with as well, that is, theological disagreement. There are many points of the faith we do not agree on, and we often believe those points to be important to the integrity of the faith. We recognize our disagreements as serious. We may be very polite about the language we use to describe one another's views, but we do not like the kind of ecumenism that is sometimes called "lowest common denominator ecumenism" or "the ecumenism of compromise."

I have been struck by what seems to me an undeniable fact: ecumenism in the past often has led to the watering down of Christian conviction and the entry of theological secularism. The reason appears to be rooted in the way in which points and principles of disagreement have been built into the foundations of our different systems of doctrine. If we try to eliminate the points and principles of disagreement, we usually end up undermining the whole system without realizing it. I believe that such an effect could be avoided; or, to put it a different way, that dialogue ecumenism could be done successfully and not undermine basic beliefs in the various churches and traditions. That, however, goes beyond the scope of this paper. Here I only wish to make clear that I am not talking about this type of ecumenism.

I would like to call to mind an important distinction here. Ecumenism has too often meant something which happens between the officials of church bodies and which is carried out by officially appointed theologians dialoguing with one another. There is, however, another kind of ecumenism, sometimes known as cooperative ecumenism, that proceeds on a different basis. It is a kind that has flourished increasingly in the last fifteen years in this country, sometimes in an irresponsible way, but often in a very positive way. This is the kind of ecumenism that I am concerned with.

Cooperative ecumenism has to proceed on the presupposition that we do not have full agreement or full unity and do not expect it for some time to come. It requires that we love one another as brothers and sisters even now, looking forward to the time when the Lord will make greater unity possible, and in the meantime we will cooperate where we can and whenever we can to strengthen the worldwide Christian cause and the Christian people. The rule should be: whatever builds up, that we will try to do. Sometimes that rule indicates not cooperating in certain ways, though we might be personally ready for them, because of the need to take into account others who do not see things our way or to avoid worsening relations between the churches. Nonetheless, the spirit behind such an approach is to seek to lay down our lives for all those whom we recognize as true brothers and sisters in Christ, and with them to advance the cause of Christ. That, I am proposing, is the proper basis of cooperation.

Dialogue ecumenism and cooperative ecumenism proceed on two different bases, practically speaking. Dialogue ecumenism proceeds on the basis that we need to discuss our differences and try to seek agreement. Cooperative ecumenism proceeds on the basis that we will cooperate where we can in matters of common concern, even though we have disagreements. That does not mean we do not talk about them. Often one of the most helpful things we can do is to educate one another in our differences so that we do not presuppose something that we should not. It certainly does not mean that we regard the differences as unimportant. But the purpose of coming together is not to work out the differences but to love one another as brothers and sisters and work together in spite of the differences.

Cooperative ecumenism proceeds, when effective, on certain principles:

1. We need to accept the fact that there are issues that divide the churches, and we need to abide by the limits that our churches have set. We cannot solve fundamental interchurch problems and should probably not try to. Nor should we act as though they did not exist. We therefore have to accept that each of us will believe the doctrines of our church and be faithful to its essential practices and current discipline.

2. In our sharing together we will emphasize the central core of Christian teaching and practice which we share in common. We will do this partly because these truths in themselves call for such emphasis. But we will also emphasize the common central core of Christian truth because we can thereby foster our unity and serve the convergence of the entire Christian people.

3. In discussing our differences together, we should
—aim at having the peace in our relationships which will

enable us to discuss differences in a loving manner
—avoid discussing those things we cannot yet discuss peacefully, gradually widening the circle of the things we can discuss as we experience the peace and trust to do so
—not be embarrassed by our own beliefs, nor be apologetic about them
—regard the things other Christians hold that we disagree with as mistakes a good Christian could make rather than as wrongdoing or a denial of Christianity
—not discuss our beliefs in a polemical way, but state them in the way that would be most acceptable to others
—ask whether the discussion is building up love and unity in the body of Christ or tearing it down.
4. We should learn about points of doctrinal and theological dispute
a. so that we can avoid expressing ourselves in ways unacceptable to others because of doctrinal commitments in certain circumstances such as:
—leading in common prayer
—proposing a common course of action
—stating an opinion that we think the group as a whole should hold
b. so that we can educate one another in our differences when that would be helpful.
5. When we can, we will talk together, help one another, and serve one another, so that we prevent our theological and cultural differences from poisoning our brotherly love, and so that our personal unity can provide the basis for a more complete unity among the whole Christian people. The cultural obstacle to our cooperation is a human one. To describe it, I want to rely on an analysis of Christopher Dawson, the British historian. It comes from a book he wrote during World War II called *The Judgment of the Nations,* a book that I personally regard as prophetic. The book was written to state the program of a movement that developed during the war called the Sword of the Spirit. Dawson summarized the goal of the movement in the following words: "What we must look for is not the alliance

of temporal power, as in the old Christendom, and an external conformity to Christian standards, but a re-ordering of all the elements of human life and civilization by the power of the Spirit: the birth of a true community which is neither an inorganic mass of individuals nor a mechanized organization of power, but a living spiritual order."[3]

One of the concerns of the Sword of the Spirit was to bring together Catholics and Protestants in Britain in a common response to the crisis of the hour, a crisis that the leaders could see was a crisis for Christian society. Ecumenical cooperation of that sort was not common then. In advocating what he called a "return to Christian unity," Dawson gave a helpful analysis of some of the main roots of disunity.

> The fundamental problem of Christian disunity is the problem of schism. In practice this problem is so closely associated with that of heresy, i.e. differences of religious belief, that they are apt to be confused with one another. But it is nevertheless important to distinguish them carefully, and to consider the nature of schism in itself, for I believe that it is in the question of schism rather than that of heresy that the key to the problem of disunity of Christendom is to be found. For heresy as a rule is not the cause of schism but an excuse for it, or rather a rationalization of it. Behind every heresy lies some kind of social conflict, and it is only by the resolution of this conflict that unity can be restored.[4]

He based his view on a historical analysis of the history of divisions among Christians.

> But, whatever view we may take of the causes of any particular schism and the social significance of particular religious movements, there can, I think, be no question but that in the history of Christendom from the Patristic period down to modern times, heresy and schism have derived their main impulse from sociological causes, so that a statesman who found a way to satisfy the national aspirations of the

Czechs in the fifteenth century, or those of the Egyptians in the fifth, would have done more to reduce the centrifugal force of the Hussite or the Monophysite movements than a theologian who made the most brilliant and convincing defence of Communion in One Kind or of the doctrine of the two natures of Christ. Whereas it is very doubtful if the converse is true, for even if the Egyptians had accepted the doctrine of Chalcedon they would have found some other ground of division so long as the sociological motive for division remained unaltered.[5]

Further on, Dawson draws this conclusion:

It is, above all, necessary to free the religious issue of all the extraneous motives that take their rise in unconscious social conflicts, for if we can do this, we shall deprive the spirit of schism of its dynamic force. If we can understand the reason for our instinctive antipathy to other religious bodies, we shall find that the purely religious and theological obstacles to reunion become less formidable and more easy to remove. But so long as the unconscious element of social conflict remains unresolved, religion is at the mercy of the blind forces of hatred and suspicion which may assume really pathological forms.[6]

Dawson goes somewhat farther in the weight he attributes to the sociological factors than I would, but, nonetheless, he puts his finger on what, in my observation, is a core difficulty in matters of Christian unity—personal relations difficulties. When two groups of people, be they nations or smaller groups, come into conflict in such a way that they desire to separate from one another, they become open to theological disagreements. They *desire* to believe differently. This is the principle behind the schism of Jeroboam and the altar at Bethel. Hence, when we are dealing with the ecumenical problem, we are dealing with intercommunity and intercultural suspicion and hostility as well as theological issues. And insofar as there is a spiritual problem at the base of the human relations problem, it can well be described as schism. The cause of schism is putting something human above Christ as the point of unity and division in our personal relations, so that we join with and separate from others over something other than faithfulness to Christ.

I believe there is a solution to this aspect of the problem of Christian unity, and the solution is our common commitment to Christ. It lies in together putting our commitment to Christ and to the cause of Christ in the world over everything else. It lies, practically speaking, in that cooperation we are discussing. It lies in working together in practical ways to strengthen one another in Christianity and in working together in practical ways to defend Christianity and to bring the world to Christ. It lies, in short, in the opposite approach to the kind of ecumenism I think so many of us dislike. The other ecumenism tries to unite Christians in a common dedication to accommodation to the world and to secular goals. Unity comes from putting aside an explicit focus on Christ and with it all the theological differences that come from different teaching about Christ and his work. For us, however, ecumenism should be a matter of restoring Christ to the center as Lord and working together where and as we can until he expands our unity. The basis of cooperation, I propose, is our core Christian commitment, one that Orthodox, Protestants, and Catholics have in common.

We are in an era in which the world is putting a question to us. In many countries, faithfulness to Christianity involves loss of wealth, position, and life. Historians tell us that our age has more martyrs than any other. And for the most part Christians are given a choice: they *can* accommodate. They can compromise without even giving up everything involved in Christianity, and thereby avoid personal loss and death. They are told, for instance, that if they are simply willing to work for the common good, the collective, the nation, and put aside their otherwordly preoccupations and divisive concerns, they do not have to experience any penalties. As near as I can see, in such situations the theological secularists tend to find ways to accommodate. They do not die for Christ. On the other hand, true Orthodox, evangelicals, and Catholics frequently find themselves undergoing the same persecution at the hands of the same persecutors.

Facing death brings one to a peculiar clarity about what is important in life. I propose, then, as the basis for our cooperation, the willingness to die for our Lord Jesus Christ. Cannot those of us who pray for the grace to be able to die for him, if it comes our way, recognize one another as brothers and sisters in him? Can we not work together for him until such time as the world puts the final question to us too, and we are called on to witness to him with our lives?

SIX

Steps to the Renewal of the Christian People

James I. Packer

The Task and the Method

In the following presentation I address myself to a twofold task: first, to formulate a clear view of what the renewal of the church really is, and then to say what needs to happen in order to get us there, starting from where we are. And in tackling that twofold task I have a twofold goal: to speak both to your minds and to your hearts. For I shall try, not just to state God's truth, but also to apply it by way of challenging your concern and your action. So, as I hope that this will not be less than a responsible theological discourse, I also hope that it will be more than that. I intend, you see, not just to lecture but also to preach.

Who am I, you may ask, to set myself this agenda? Let me tell you. I am an expatriate Englishman, an Episcopal pastor by calling and a Reformed theologian by trade, who in 1945, soon after his conversion, was given a copy of Charles G. Finney's *Lectures on Revivals of Religion* (1835), and who since that time has carried a personal burden of concern for the renewing of God's people through a fresh outpouring of the Holy Spirit. On this subject I have spoken repeatedly, written occasionally, and thought constantly throughout those years. Now I seek to enlist you for the pursuit of the same interest, and I am grateful for the opportunity to do so.

There is, however, one thing that I need to say at the very

outset about the manner of pursuing an interest of this kind. Renewal in all its aspects is not a theme for dilettante debate, but for humble, penitent, prayerful, faith-full exploration before the Lord, with a willingness to change and be changed, and if necessary to be the first to be changed, if that is what the truth proves to require. To absorb ideas about renewal ordinarily costs nothing, but to enter into renewal could cost us everything we have, and we shall be very guilty if, having come to understand renewal, we then decline it. We need to be clear about that. John Calvin once declared that it would be better for a preacher to break his neck while mounting the pulpit if he did not himself intend to be the first to follow God.[1] In the same way, it would be better for us not to touch the study of renewal at all if we are not ourselves ready to be the first to be renewed. I speak as to wise men; please judge what I say.

By what method, now, shall we approach our subject? Here the gates of two "by-path meadows," to use Bunyan's phrase, stand invitingly open. First, it is tempting to come at the renewal theme *sociologically*. That would mean defining "the Christian people" in external and institutional terms, as an organized association with specific goals; equating renewal with the achieving of those goals; and then occupying ourselves in pragmatic reflection on what structural and attitudinal changes would have to be engineered in order to realize these goals in a statistically measurable way. The idea that the church's health problems can be solved by such manipulation is not unfamiliar, at least to members of major Protestant denominations in North America; analysts both inside and outside denominational headquarters do a great deal of thinking at this level. Nor do I dismiss such analysis as useless; on the contrary, it does much to make us aware of lacks and needs in the church's life. But I urge most emphatically that the renewal of the church is in essence a spiritual and supernatural matter, a work of the Holy Spirit enriching our fellowship with the Father and the Son, and it takes more than clever social engineering to bring this about.

Again, it is tempting to come at our theme *historically*. That would mean identifying past movements of renewal and revival, from the Old Testament records of Israel's return to Yahweh under Asa, Hezekiah, Josiah, Ezra, and others, and the New Testament story in Acts of revival in Palestine after Pentecost, through to the Cistercian and Dominican and Franciscan movements; the ministry of Savonarola; the Western Reformation; the early Jesuits; English Puritanism and Lutheran Pietism; the Evangelical Awakenings in old England and New England in the eighteenth century; the repeated stirrings of the Spirit in Wales and Scotland between the seventeenth and nineteenth centuries; the first hundred years of the Protestant missionary movement; the frontier revivals in America; The worldwide quickenings among Protestants in the 1850s and again in the 1900s; the East African revival, now fifty years old and still continuing; the awakenings in Lewis, off the west coast of Scotland, in the 1950s, in Western Canada in the 1960s, and in Indonesia and the Californian "Jesus movement" in the 1970s; the impact of the worldwide charismatic movement over the past twenty years; and so on. It would then mean analyzing, comparing, reconstructing, and characterizing these movements in the way that historians do, and seeking to produce out of this exercise generalized typologies of renewal for future reference. Now I do not wish to minimize the very great value of this kind of study. The psalmists charge us to keep God's mighty works in remembrance, and we should be glad that in our day so much printed material on past renewal movements is available to us.[2] But if all we did was study renewal historically, we should in the first place be looking at it in a merely external and this-worldly way, as the phenomenon of changed outlooks and activities in certain persons' lives, and in the second place we could hardly avoid lapsing into what I call the antiquarian fallacy about renewal, the assumption, that is, that any future renewal will become recognizable by conforming to some pattern set in the past. That there are such patterns is not in doubt; they merit careful examination, and in that connection I commend in particular Richard Lovelace's pioneer theological phenomenology of renewal, *Dynamics of Spiritual Life* (1979). But we should limit God improperly, and actually quench the

Spirit, if we assumed that future movements of renewal will correspond in outward form to some past movement, and that we can rely on this correspondence as a means of identifying them. Renewal is precisely God doing a new thing, and though as we shall see every work of renewal has basic qualities, or dimensions, in common with every other, we must recognize that the contours of the cultures within which the church has from time to time lost its vitality, and also the contours of that loss in itself, have varied; which means that it is not safe for us to assume that the outward forms and phenomena of revival in this or any future age will always prove to have exact historical precedents. At this point sad mistakes in judgment have been made in the past, and I suspect are being made by some in the present. Let us strive not to be of their number.

What I have said makes it apparent, I hope, that our basic need in studying renewal is for categories and criteria that are neither sociological nor historical but theological, which for me at least means biblically based. With scripture as our guide, therefore, we shall now discuss, first, the *theology* of renewal (that is, the overall account that should be given of renewal as a work of God); second, the *elements* in renewal (that is, specific things that occur when this work of God is in progress); third, the *quest* for renewal (that is, the steps in seeking renewal which we and the segments of the body of Christ to which we belong could take, starting now).

The Theology of Renewal

For some decades the word "renewal" has been used loosely in the world church, with applications as wide as they are unfocused. The general sense that renewal is needed because the church is not all that it should be is welcome, but the vague way in which the word is thrown around is unhelpful, to say the least. Contemporary voices celebrate liturgical renewal, theological renewal, lay renewal, ecumenical renewal, charismatic renewal, and renewal in other departments too; indeed, it seems that any new outburst of activity in the church, any cloud of dust raised by the stamping of excited feet, will be hailed as renewal by somebody. Certainly, there is no renewal without activity, and when renewal is a reality every area of the church's life should benefit. But the implicit equating of renewal with enthusiasm and activity is inadequate in two ways. First, it gives an idea of renewal which is far too *inclusive*: horizontally, so to speak, it embraces too much. For in biblical thought and experience renewal is linked with divine visitation, purging judgment, and restoration through repentance, and no amount of hustle and bustle qualifies as renewal where these notes are absent. Second, this equation gives an idea of renewal which is far too *superficial*: vertically, so to speak, it does not include enough. It views renewal in terms of externals only, and takes no account of the inward exercise of heart in encounter with God in which true renewal as scripture depicts it always begins. But hustle and bustle do not constitute renewal apart from this inward dimension.

How then should we define renewal? The word is one of a group—spiritual, renewal, revival, awakening, visitation, reformation—which tend to be used together and need to be defined together. Five of these six are correlated by Richard Lovelace in a way which both corresponds to usage and clarifies the realities involved. I quote him. "*Spiritual* (as in *spiritual life, spiritual gifts*) . . . means *deriving from the Holy Spirit,* which is its normal significance in scripture. *Renewal, revival,* and *awakening* trace back to biblical metaphors for the infusion of spiritual life in Christian experience by the Holy Spirit (see Rom 6:4, 8:2-11; Eph 1:17-23, 3:14-19, 5:14). Usually they are used synonymously for broad-scale movements of the Holy Spirit's work in renewing spiritual vitality in the church and in fostering its expansion in mission and evangelism. *Reformation* refers to the purifying of doctrine and structures in the church, but implies also a component of spiritual revitalization. *Renewal* is sometimes used to encompass revival and reformation, and also to include *aggiornamento,* the updating of the church leading to a new engagement with the surrounding world."[3] To Lovelace's definitions I add that *visitation,* the sixth word in the group, signifies the initial divine approach to spiritually moribund communities out of which their renewal comes.

Lovelace's two definitions of *renewal* alert us to the fact that this is one of those "concertina-words" which in use keep alternating between a narrower and a broader significance. The term carries its narrowest meaning (concertina closed) when it is used of the personal quickening of an individual. Used so, it signifies that his spiritual life—that is, his God-given fellowship with the Father and the Son through the Spirit, the saving relationship which finds expression in his praise and prayer, his devotion and character, his work and his witness—has been decisively deepened through God's visiting his soul. ("His," by the way, in that last sentence includes "hers"; I am not suggesting that only males experience personal renewal!) At the other end of the scale, *renewal* has its broadest meaning (concertina open) when it is applied to the church, for here, in idea at any rate, it signifies revitalizing at every level, starting with believers' inner lives (what Puritans called their "heart-work") and extending to all the characteristic public activities in which the body of Christ is called to engage. Following the thrust of the definite article in my assigned title when it speaks of "renewal of *the* Christian people," I focus in this paper on the latter, broader application of the word. You cannot, of course, have corporate renewal of any part of the body of Christ on earth without personal renewal of those who make it up, although the quickening of individuals can and does constantly occur without it being part of any larger local movement; but here I shall speak of personal renewal only in the context of corporate renewal, the quickening of "the Christian people" in this place or that.

In terms of biblical theology, now, we can characterize God's work of renewal in the following three ways.

First, renewal is an *eschatological* reality, in the sense that it is a general experiential deepening of that life in the Spirit which is the foretaste and first installment of heaven itself. Assurance of both the shameful guiltiness and the total pardon of our sins; joy, humble but exalted, in the awareness of God's love for us;

knowledge of the closeness of the Father and the Son in both communion and affection; a never-ending passion to praise God; an abiding urge to love, serve, and honor the Father, the Son, the Spirit, and the saints, and inward freedom to express that urge creatively and spontaneously—these things will be the essence of the life of heaven, and they are already the leading marks of spiritually renewed individuals and communities in this world. To describe situations of renewal, as Protestants, using the word *revival,* are prone to do, as heaven on earth is not devotional hyperbole; intrinsically and ontologically, that is exactly what the renewal of the Christian people is.

Second, renewal is a *Christological* reality, in two ways. First, it is *subjectively* Christocentric, in the sense that awareness of the gracious, beneficent personal presence of the glorified Lord Jesus—"Jesus, my Shepherd, Husband, Friend, my Prophet, Priest and King, my Lord, my life, my way, my end," as Newton's marvellous hymn puts it; Jesus, who guards, guides, keeps, and feeds me, and finally receives me to be with him forever in glory, is the very heart of the renewed Christian's sense of reality. The vision of Christ's glory, the realization that every one of God's good gifts comes to us through him and the passion to love and adore him, come to pervade the minds and hearts of persons in renewal to a degree that is a major anticipation of heaven, as was said in the last paragraph. The lady who explained to me her identification with a certain renewal movement by saying, "I just want the Lord Jesus to run my life," could not have been better directed: she was after the right thing, and she was looking for it in the right place. It is precisely in renewal that love to Jesus and fellowship with him become most clear-sighted and deep. The most obvious evidence of this is the hymnology of renewal movements. Charles Wesley was the supreme poet of love to Jesus in a revival context: think of his "Jesus, lover of my soul," and the final stanzas of "Thou hidden source of calm repose"—

Jesus, my all in all thou art,
    My rest in toil, my ease in pain,

The medicine of my broken heart,
    In war my peace, in loss my gain,
My smile beneath the tyrant's frown,
    In shame my glory and my crown;
In want my plentiful supply,
    In weakness my almighty power,
In bonds my perfect liberty,
    My light in Satan's darkest hour,
In grief my joy unspeakable,
    My life in death, my heaven in hell.

Or think of this, from the supreme preacher of love to Christ in a renewal context, Bernard of Clairvaux:

Jesus, the very thought of thee
    With sweetness fills my breast;
But sweeter far thy face to see,
    And in thy presence rest.
O hope of every contrite heart,
    O joy of all the meek,
To those who fall how kind thou art!
    How good to those who seek!
But what to those who find? Ah! this
    Nor tongue nor pen can show:
The love of Jesus, what it is,
    None but his loved ones know.
Jesus, our only joy be thou,
    As thou our prize wilt be;
Jesus, be thou our glory now
    And through eternity.

One mark of spiritual authenticity in the renewal songs of our time—Christian camp fire songs, as they have sometimes been called—is that in them the theme of Christ's love to us and ours to him surfaces once more, and strongly.

Second, renewal is *objectively* Christocentric, in the sense that through it believers are drawn deeper into their baptismal life of dying with Christ in repentance and self-denial and rising with him into the new righteousness of combating sin and living in obedience to God. Authentic revivals have deep ethical effects; they produce authentic sanctity—really, though not always uniformly, tidily, or calmly—along with authentic ministry one to another; and both these features of authentic Christianity should be viewed as the supernatural life of Christ himself living and serving in and through his members by means of the operation of the Spirit. Also, the intensified communion with Christ should be seen as based upon the dynamic reality of this our union with him—or, better, this his union with us.

The third point in the biblical concept of renewal is that it is a *pneumatological* reality, in the sense that it is through the action of the Holy Spirit doing his New Covenant work of glorifying the glorified Christ before the eyes of the understanding of his disciples, as was described above, that renewal actually takes place. Here, incidentally, is a sure test of whether particular stirrings of excitement about interior experience of God are instances of Holy Spirit renewal or not: as Jonathan Edwards argued against critics of the Great Awakening, it is not the devil who exalts Christ, but the Holy Spirit, so that if the experiences in question deepen Christ-centered devotion, that proves their source. And if they do not, that proves their source too. For Satan's strategy is always to distract men from Christ, and getting them to concentrate on exotic experiences—visions, voices, thrills, drug trips, and all the mumbo-jumbo of false mysticism and nonrational meditation—is as good a way for him to do it as any other.

In addition to characterizing renewal in this way, biblical theology answers for us the question, what place has renewal in God's overall purposes? "Restore us again, O God of our salvation," prays the psalmist, "and put away thy indignation toward us! Wilt thou be angry with us for ever? Wilt thou prolong thy anger to all generations? Wilt thou not revive us again, that thy people may rejoice in thee?" (Ps 85:4-6). Those verses, which can be matched from many passages in the psalms and the prophets, beg for a quickening visitation to the community ("restore, or revive, *us* again") which will have a twofold experiential significance. First, this reviving will be experienced as *the ending of God's wrath,* the termination of the impotence, frustration, and barrenness which have been the tokens of divine displeasure for unfaithfulness. Second, this reviving will be experienced as *the exulting of God's people*: joy will replace the distress which knowledge of God's displeasure has made the faithful feel. Then, third, as appears most clearly from the Acts narrative, such reviving is also experienced as *the extending of God's kingdom.* God's visitation to renew his own household regularly has an evangelistic and cultural overflow, often of great power, leading to the fulfillment in churchly terms of what Zechariah foresaw in terms of the post-exilic restoration: "Ten men from the nations of every tongue shall take hold of the robe of the Jew, saying 'Let us go with you, for we have heard that God is with you'" (Zech 8:23). Again and again, for the glory of God in and through his church, this pattern of events has needed to recur, and has in fact recurred, both in and since the biblical period.

In *Dynamics of Spiritual Life,* Dr. Lovelace argues that the apparent antithesis between the two models of cyclical and continuous renewal which the Old and New Testaments respectively seem to throw up is not absolute since the same spiritual forces operate in both types of situations.[4] I agree, and to clarify the point I offer a distinction between *renewing* or *reviving* as an act of God—that is, the initial visitation which sparks off a new movement—and *revival* or *renewal* itself—that is, the state of revivedness in which God's people continue until for whatever cause the power of the original visitation is withdrawn. Thus one may say that Pentecost was a day of renewing; that renewal conditions surrounded all the protagonists of the church history recorded in Acts, as the New Testament letters also show by the quality of the devotional experience to which they testify; but that six of the seven churches of the Apocalypse had quenched the Spirit, so that the quality of their inward responsiveness to Jesus Christ was now noticeably reduced, and repentance on their part and a fresh visitation from their Lord was urgently needed. How this might bear on the present life of our own churches, and on our own roles and responsibilities within them, is something at which we must look with some care. But first we should spend a moment reviewing the *elements* in revival, which I announced as the second part of our discussion.

The Elements in Renewal

The phenomena of renewal movements merit much more study by church historians, theologians, and exponents of Christian spirituality than they have yet received. At surface level, they vary widely, as do the movements within which they appear, and we should not be surprised at that. For, in the first place, spiritual movements are partly shaped by preexisting needs, which in their turn reflect all sorts of nonrecurring cultural and economic factors, as well as many aspects of the morbid pathology of sin and spiritual decline; and, in the second place, the spiritual experiences of Christians are determined in part by temperament, by atmosphere, and by pressure groups, all of which are variables; and, in the third place, God the Lord appears to delight in variety and never quite repeats himself. But at the level of deeper analysis, deeper, that is, than verbal and cultural variants and preset interpretative grids, there are constant factors recognizable in all biblical and post-biblical revivals and renewals of faith and life, whatever their historical, racial, and cultural settings. They number five, as follows: awareness of God's presence; responsiveness to God's word; sensitiveness to sin; liveliness in community; fruitfulness in testimony. Let me illustrate them briefly.

(1) Awareness of God's presence. The first and fundamental feature in renewal is the sense that God has drawn awesomely near in his holiness, mercy, and might. This is felt as the fulfilling of the prayer of Isaiah 64:1f: "O that thou wouldst rend the heavens and come down, that the mountains might quake at thy presence . . . to make thy name known to thine adversaries, and that the nations may tremble at thy presence." God "comes," "visits" his people, and makes his majesty known. The effect is regularly as it was for Isaiah himself, when he "saw the Lord sitting on a throne" in the temple and heard the angels" song—"Holy, holy, holy"—and was forced to cry, "Woe is me, for I am ruined! Because I am a man of unclean lips, and I live among a people of unclean lips" (Is 6:1-5). It is with this searching, scorching manifestation of God's presence that renewal begins, and by its continuance that renewal is sustained. Says Arthur Wallis: "The spirit of revival is the consciousness of God."⁵ Wrote Duncan Campbell, out of his experience of revival in Lewis from 1949 to 1953: "I have no hesitation in saying that this awareness of God is the crying need of the church today."⁶ This, and nothing less than this, is what the outpouring of the Spirit in renewal means in experiential terms.

(2) Responsiveness to God's word. The sense of God's presence imparts new authority to his truth. The message of scripture which previously was making only a superficial impact, if that, now searches its hearers and readers to the depth of their being. The statement that "the word of God is living and active, sharper than any two-edged sword, piercing to the division of soul and spirit, of joints and marrow, and discerning the thoughts and intents of the heart" (Heb 4:12) is verified over and over again. Paul thanked God that when the Thessalonians heard from the missionaries "the word of God . . . you accepted it not as the word of men but as what it really is, the word of God" (1 Thes 2:13). They did because "our gospel did not come to you in word, but also in power and in the Holy Spirit and with full conviction" (1:5). It is always so in renewal times. God's message—the gospel call to repentance, faith, and holiness, to praise and prayer, witness and worship—authenticates itself unambiguously to men's consciences, and there is no room for half measures in response. That leads to our next point.

(3) Sensitiveness to sin. Deep awareness of what things are sinful and how sinful we ourselves are—*conviction* of sin, to use the old phrase—is the third phenomenon of renewal that calls for notice. No upsurge of religious interest or excitement merits the name of renewal if there is no deep sense of sin at its heart. God's coming, and the consequent impact of his word, makes Christians much more sensitive to sin than they previously were: consciences become tender and a profound humbling takes place. The gospel of forgiveness through Christ's cross comes to be loved as never before, when folk see their need of it so much more clearly. That conviction of sin was very much part of the early Christian story, and the opening chapters of Acts give us three examples of it.

In Acts 2:37-41 we see conviction *accepted.* Peter's congregation was "pierced to the heart" (2:37) with a sense of their guilt for compassing Jesus' death. The Greek word for "pierced" means literally to inflict a violent blow; it is a painfully vivid image for what was an acutely painful experience. Shattered, the congregation cried out, "Brethren, what shall we do?" Peter showed them the way of faith, repentance, and discipleship, and three thousand of them took it. Thus, conviction was the means of their blessing.

In Acts 7:54-60 we see conviction *resisted.* Stephen has accused his Jewish judges of resisting the Spirit, murdering the Christ, and showing contempt for the law (7:51-53). They are "cut to the quick" (7:54)—the Greek word literally means "sawn apart"; it expresses the inner turmoil arising from the conjunction of inescapable guilt and uncontrollable anger. Too proud to admit they had been wrong, they ground their teeth, yelled at Stephen, stopped their ears, mobbed him, ran him out of town, and stoned him to death. The trauma of felt guilt had driven them into hysteria. Conviction in this case was the means of their hardening.

Then in Acts 5:1-10 we see conviction *killing*—literally. Peter tells Ananias that he has lied to the Holy Spirit and so to God, and Ananias dies. A divine judgment, certainly; but what account of it should we give in human terms? The most natural view is that in that revitalized community, where sensitiveness to the presence of God and hence to the foulness of sin was exceedingly strong, the realization of what he had done so overwhelmed Ananias that his frame could not stand it, and he died of shock; and Sapphira the same. They literally could not live with their sin. Thus, conviction became the means of their judgment.

What do we learn from this? That under revival conditions consciences are so quickened that conviction of sin becomes strong and terrible, inducing agonies of mind that are beyond imagining till they happen. But conviction of sin is a means, not an end; the Spirit of God convinces of sin in order to induce repentance, and one of the more striking features of renewal movements is the depth of repentance into which both saints and sinners are led. Repentance, as we know, is basically not moaning and remorse, but turning and change: "about turn, quick march" is a good formula to express its meaning. In 2 Corinthians 7:10, Paul says, "The sorrow that is according to the will of God produces a repentance without regret, leading to salvation," and in the next verse he applauds the robustness of the Corinthians' repentance in the matter about which he had rebuked them. "What earnestness . . . this godly sorrow has produced in you: what vindication of yourselves, what indignation, what fear, what longing, what zeal, what avenging of wrong!" Vivid conviction produces vigorous repentance.

In times of renewal the impulse constantly recurs, often in defiance of cultural conditioning, to signalize and seal one's repentance by public confession of what one is renouncing: as was done at Ephesus, apparently spontaneously, when "many . . . of those who had believed kept coming, confessing and disclosing their practices" (Acts 19:18), and some occult practitioners went so far as publicly to burn their very valuable books of spells—a costly and humbling gesture, no doubt, but equally certainly a liberating one for those who made it. One or more of three motives prompts public confession. It is partly for *purgation*: individuals feel that the only way to get evil things off their conscience and out of their lives is by renouncing them publicly. Sins are also confessed for *healing* (Jas 5:16): pocketing pride and admitting one's faults and failings to others is part of God's therapy. And, finally, sins are confessed for *doxology*: "Come and hear, all who fear God, and I will tell of what He has done for my soul" (Ps 66:16). This kind of confession is likely to appear spontaneously wherever there is genuine renewal.

(4) Liveliness in community. Love and generosity, unity and joy, assurance and boldness, a spirit of praise and prayer, and a passion to reach out to win others are recurring marks of renewed communities. So is divine power in their preachers, a power which has nothing to do with natural eloquence. John Howe, the Puritan, once Cromwell's chaplain, spoke of this in a passage in a sermon on Ezekiel 39:29 ("I have poured out my Spirit upon the house of Israel, saith the Lord God"). Preaching in 1678 and looking back on the great days of the Puritan revival under the Commonwealth, he told his congregation:

When the Spirit shall be poured forth plentifully . . . I believe you will hear much other kind of sermons . . . than you are wont to do now-a-days. . . . It is plain, too sadly plain, that there is a great retraction of the Spirit of God even from us. We [preachers] know not how to speak living sense [= *sensus*, a feeling, felt reality] unto souls, how to get within you; our words die in our mouths, or drop and die between you and us. We even faint, when we speak; long experienced unsuccessfulness makes us despond. We speak not as persons that hope to prevail, that expect to make you more serious, heavenly, mindful of God, and to walk more like Christians. . . . When such an effusion of the Spirit shall be as is here signified . . . ministers . . . shall know how to speak to better purpose, with more compassion and sense, with more seriousness, with more authority and allurement, than we now find we can.[7]

Also in renewal times God acts quickly: his work accelerates. When Paul left Thessalonika after between two and three weeks' ministry there he left behind him a virile church whose quality can be gauged from 1 Thessalonians 1-3. God had moved fast. No wonder Paul asks them to pray that "the word of the Lord may speed on [literally, run] and triumph, as it did among you" (2 Thes 3:1). Truth spreads, and people are born again and grow in Christ, with amazing rapidity under renewal conditions.

(5) Fruitfulness in testimony. Revival of the church always has an evangelistic and ethical overspill into the world: Christians proclaim by word and deed the power of the new life, souls are won, and a community conscience informed by Christian values emerges.

Such in outline is the constant pattern by which genuine movements of renewal identify themselves. Christians in renewal are accordingly found living in God's presence (*coram Deo*), attending to his word, feeling acute concern about sin and righteousness, rejoicing in the assurance of Christ's love and their own salvation, spontaneously constant in worship, and tirelessly active in witness and service, fuelling these activities by praise and prayer. The question that presses, therefore, is not whether renewal is approved as a theological idea or claimed as a shibboleth of fashion (to say "we are in renewal" is almost mandatory in some circles nowadays). The question that presses is whether renewal is actually displayed in the lives of Christian individuals and communities: whether this quality of Christian life is there or not. Which brings us to our final section.

The Quest for Renewal

This is where analysis finally merges into application and lecturing becomes preaching. I have three points to develop: First, our guilt in not being renewed, and God's call to us to repent of it; second, our inability to renew ourselves, and God's call to us to seek renewal from him; third, our obligation to remove obstacles to our being renewed, and God's call to us to act now in this matter. What this amounts to is a summons to us all to be more honest with God, more simple and thoroughgoing in our response to his grace, more open and straightforward both with him and with others, than we may have been hitherto. Let me try to spell this out as I understand it.

Theme one: our guilt in not being renewed, and God's call to us to repent of it. For this I need only refer you once more to the letters of our Lord to the seven churches of the Revelation. With only one of them, the Philadelphian congregation, was the Savior pleased; the Ephesian church was condemned for having left its first love (2:4f), the church at Sardis for being dead (3:1), and the church at Laodicia for being self-satisfied and self-deceived. "I know your works," says Jesus to them; "you are neither cold nor hot. Would that you were cold or hot! So, because you are lukewarm, and neither cold nor hot, I will spew you out of my mouth. For you say, I am rich, I have prospered, and I need nothing; not knowing that you are wretched, pitiable, poor, blind, and naked. . . . Those whom I love I rebuke and chasten; so be zealous and repent" (3:15-17, 19). It is hard to doubt that this is the mind of Jesus with regard to many churches in North America today.

Biblical theology knows no middle condition, for churches or for Christians, between spiritual advance under God's blessing and spiritual decline under his displeasure. The root of spiritual decline is always human unfaithfulness in some form, and its fruit is always chastening judgment from God, whose gracious plan and supernatural enabling are hereby slighted and dishonored. Marks of decline include high tolerance of half-heartedness, moral failure, and compromise; low expectations of holiness in oneself and others; willingness to remain Christian pigmies; apathy about the advancement of God's cause and his glory; and contentment, even complacency, with things as they are. Charles Finney once said, "Christians are more to blame for not being revived, than sinners are for not being converted."[8] Was he right? It is, at the very least, a question worth thinking about as we reflect on the relevance to ourselves of Jesus' words to the Laodiceans. And perhaps in doing this we shall need to make our own the words of the Anglican litany: "from hardness of heart, and contempt of thy word and commandment, good Lord, deliver us."

So we move to theme two: our inability to renew ourselves, and our need to seek this blessing from God by prayer. The point here is that whereas self-reliance, expressing self-sufficiency, is natural (we might almost say, instinctive) to us in our fallenness, it is beyond us to compass spiritual renewal by any form of activity that we organize. The principle is that underlying Isaiah 22:8-14, where Judah's feverish bustle of defensive activity in face of trouble was ruling out anything in the nature of a genuine return to God and a genuine dependence on him for the deliverance which only he could give. To look to human ingenuity, however, for that which only God in his grace can give is arrogant, inept, and in the outcome barren. And that is how it is in the matter of renewal. When Christians, by the Laodicean character of their lives and their ecclesiastical systems, have quenched the fire of God's Spirit, and so brought about a withdrawal of God's presence and glory, it is beyond their power to kindle the fire again, much as they might wish to do so; only God himself, by his own quickening visitation, can renew, and for this we have to wait on him in patient, persistent, penitent prayer until he is pleased to act. Charles Finney, who for a decade after his conversion was used by God in a continuous revival ministry, came to think, evidently generalizing from that experience, that self-examination and earnest prayer on a congregation's part would always secure a divine visitation and fresh outpouring of the Spirit immediately. But the experience of many who have sought to implement this formula, and indeed the different and disappointing experience of Finney himself in later years, shows that this is not so. In no situation can revival be infallibly predicted or precipitated; there are no natural laws of renewal for man the manager to discover and exploit. That, however is no cause for discouragement, for the other side of the coin is that the possibility of renewal can never be precluded either; no one can set limits to the graciousness of God who has promised that we shall find him when we seek him with all our hearts. To seek God and his renewing grace, recognizing that he can renew us though we cannot renew ourselves, is in this instance the only constructive thing that is open to us to do. "Ask, and it will be given you; seek, and you will find," says our Lord (Mt 7:7). The Psalter provides several pattern prayers for this purpose, notably Psalms 44, 67, 74, 79, and 85. Waiting on God in constant acknowledgment of need, pleading that he should move in mercy, is the way forward here.

Finally, we move to theme three: our obligation to remove hindrances to renewal, and God's call to us to begin doing this now. A moment ago I said that we cannot precipitate a visitation from God. That is true; God is sovereign in these matters and takes action to answer prayer at his own speed and in his own good time. Yet there is something we can do at this present moment to bring spiritual quickening nearer, and that is to break with things that are in their own nature Spirit-quenching.

For instance: surely *clericalism* as a leadership style is Spirit-quenching. Clericalism, which on my analysis involves more persons than the ordained, is a sort of conspiracy between leaders and those led: the one party (it does not matter which) says, "all spiritual ministry should be left to the leader," and the other party says, "yes, that"s right." Some leaders embrace clericalism because it gives them power; others, running scared, embrace it because they fear lest folk ministering alongside them should overshadow them, or because they feel incapable of handling an every-member-ministry situation. But every-member-ministry in the body of Christ is the New Testament pattern, and anything which obstructs or restricts it is an obstacle to a renewing visitation from God. What does this suggest that leaders, and others, ought to do now?

Again: surely *formalism* as a worship style is Spirit-quenching But many churches seem to view worship in a way that can only be called formalistic, for their interest is limited to performing set routines with suitable correctness, and there is no apparent desire on anyone's part actually to meet God. What does this suggest that leaders, and others, ought to do now?

Yet once more: surely personal attitudes of *complacency* about things as they are is Spirit-quenching. Think of your own church or fellowship: to what extent do you see in it the reality of worship? faith? repentance? knowledge? holiness? Do its members resolutely, energetically, passionately love the Lord? Do they love each other? How do they pray? How do they give? How much support do they get from each other in times of personal need? How much sharing of their faith do they do, or try to do? Ought you to be content with things as they are? Think also of yourself, and of what these folk see in you. Ought either they or you to be content with what you are? It must be expected that those led will become like their leaders; that is the natural thing to happen; but if it happens so in your church or fellowship, will that be good enough? What does this lien of thought suggest that leaders, and others, ought to do now?

The first step, perhaps, to the renewal of the Christian people is that leaders should begin to repent of their too-ready acceptance of too-low levels of attainment both in themselves and in those whom they lead, and should learn to pray from their hearts the simple-sounding but totally demanding prayer in Edwin Orr's chorus: *"send a revival—start the work in me."* The second step, perhaps, is for leaders to challenge their followers as to whether they are not too much like the Laodiceans of Revelation, and whether Jesus' searing words to these latter—"you are lukewarm. . . . you say, I need nothing; not knowing that you are wretched, pitiable, poor, blind, and naked. . . . be zealous, and repent. Behold, I stand at the door and knock. . . ."—do not apply directly to themselves, here and now. The third step, perhaps, is for us all, leaders and led together, to become more serious, expectant, and honest with each other as we look to God in our use of the means of grace—sermon and sacrament, worship and witness, praise and prayer, meditation and petition—and as we seek to make our own the psalmist's plea: "Search me, O God, and know my heart! Try me and know my thoughts! And see if there be any wicked way in me, and lead me in the way everlasting!" (Ps 139:23-24). Then the fourth step, perhaps, will be to trust the Holy Spirit to lead us on from there.

Does this prospect strike awe into you? I am sure that it does, and it has the same effect on me. But that is no justification for drawing back from it, when our need of it is so plain.

"O Lord, I have heard the report of thee, and thy work, O Lord, do I fear. In the midst of the years renew it; in the midst of the years make it known; in wrath remember mercy" (Hab 3:2).

Let all the people say: amen.

SEVEN

A Strategy for Pastoral Renewal

Mark Kinzer

SOMETHING THAT COMES FORTH clearly in Dr. Packer's message is that we cannot substitute human efforts for the action of God. There is no substitute for God coming and renewing his people. We cannot concoct an independent strategy for church renewal. At the same time it is important for us not to draw the wrong type of antithesis between God's action and our own efforts. When we understand that the goal of all of our efforts and strategies is a spiritual renewal, and when we use all of the tools that are placed at our disposal for the renewal of God's people in the power of the Holy Spirit, with prayer, then, I think, we can experience our efforts as being under the sovereign reign of God and as his instruments in the renewal of his people.

The strategy we adopt for pastoral renewal will depend largely on how we conceive of the goal of pastoral work. We could infer from the activities of many pastoral leaders that the goal of their work is to run an efficient organization—administratively trim, numerically strong, financially prosperous. Many aspire to have their congregations contribute to the broader community in the manner of a public service institution. The church or fellowship is viewed primarily as an organization with meetings to be led, services to be conducted, buildings to be maintained, schools to be run, community help projects to be staffed.

The Christian church does have an important institutional side. It is not an amorphous and unstructured aggregate of individuals. There *are* services to be conducted, buildings to be maintained, and an organizational apparatus to be administered. However, the church is much more than an institution. It is the body of the incarnate Son of God, who is its head and lives in union with it through the Holy Spirit. It is the people submitted in covenant to the Lord of Hosts and bound together in commitment, fidelity, and love. The church has important institutional elements as a consequence of its humanity, but these elements are not ends in themselves but rather means of building up the body to the fullness of its spiritual and human form—to the maturity of the new humanity, the measure of the stature of the fullness of Christ (Eph 4:13). We should not let a professional preoccupation with the organizational elements of the church obscure its more fundamental identity as the people of God.

The goal of pastoral work should relate primarily to the church as a people rather than as a network of institutions. The goal should be the living of a particular way of life. What sort of life is this? The apostle Paul states it as follows: "Only let your manner of life be *worthy of the gospel of Christ*" (Phil 1:27). In a general sense, we can say that the goal of pastoral work is to help the Christian people live in a way that is worthy of the gospel.

What does it mean to live a life worthy of the gospel of Christ? Or, to use an expression popularized by Watchman Nee, what is the normal Christian life? I would propose the following five elements as the foundation stones of the normal Christian life: commitment to Jesus Christ, life in the Holy Spirit, membership in the body, faithfulness to gospel teaching, and fruitfulness in life and service. Anyone who lacks any of these elements is lacking something essential to the Christian life. On the other hand, anyone who is strong in all of these elements is certain to be living a healthy and mature Christian life. Let us now look at each of these foundation stones to see what they actually entail.

1. Commitment to Jesus. Christianity begins and ends with Jesus Christ. Jesus is the greatest of teachers, the one who authoritatively interpreted the law of God and revealed the mysteries of the kingdom of heaven. Jesus is the greatest of prophets, the one who summoned fallen Israel back to its ancestral inheritance. Jesus is the perfect model of righteousness, fulfilling the commandments in their entirety and giving the ultimate example of self-denying love upon the cross. Even more, Jesus is the Lamb of God who shed his blood as an atoning sacrifice for the sins of the world, the risen Lord who conquered death and now sits enthroned at the Father's right hand, the incarnate Logos who dwelt in union with the Father before the foundation of the world. Commitment to Christianity means commitment to Jesus Christ, Lord of the universe.

In the New Testament the Christian life is often described as a life of discipleship to Jesus. Jesus does not call people primarily to a new teaching or an ideal of life but to a radical commitment to himself: "He who loves father or mother more than me is not worthy of me; and he who loves son or daughter more than me is not worthy of me; and he who does not take his cross and follow me is not worthy of me" (Mt 10:37-38). This discipleship involves an intense personal loyalty that implies a willingness to suffer even to the death. It involves sacrifice and self-denial. This is the call that Jesus gives to *all* who would bear his name; there are no "associate disciples" in the New Testament, no special category for those who want to support his mission but do not care to devote themselves fully to his cause and his person. The "disciples" in the New Testament *are* the church and not a special spiritual elite within the church. Discipleship is just another word for Christianity.

If we are committed to Jesus as his disciples, then loyalty to him takes precedence over all other concerns. Career, possessions, reputation, security, and even family must be subordinated to the overriding call of the Master. Our commitment to Jesus should be expressed in the way we use our money and the way we spend our time, the friends we choose and the books we read. No area of life is exempt from the lordship of Christ.

2. Life in the Holy Spirit. The normal Christian life is not only a matter of our following the Lord Jesus Christ. It is also a matter of the Lord Jesus Christ living and working in us through the Holy Spirit: "If a man loves me, he will keep my word, and my Father will love him, and we will come to him and make our home with him" (Jn 14:23). Through the Holy Spirit our lives are transformed, and we are enabled to live as disciples of Christ.

We all know that the gift of the Holy Spirit is an integral part of the creeds. We also know that one is not a full Christian if one does not have the Spirit of God (Rom 8:9b). However, not all Christians have faced the consequences of this truth. The Holy Spirit in the New Testament is more than just another point of doctrine; he is the one who applies all doctrine to our lives and makes it real and vital. We are supposed to experience the presence of the Holy Spirit in our lives and appreciate his effectual workings. The author of the book of Hebrews describes the experiential dimension of the normal Christian life as follows: "Those who have once been enlightened, who have tasted the heavenly gift, and have become partakers of the Holy Spirit, and have tasted the goodness of the word of God and the powers of the age to come . . ." (Heb 6:4-5). The light of the Holy Spirit is to be *seen,* the power to be *tasted.* The images of sensory experience are employed to convey the reality of a spiritual experience.

Many of us are justifiably cautious about an overemphasis on Christian spiritual experience. We know that it is all too easy to slide into the ocean of subjectivity that pervades our secular humanist culture. Nonetheless, scripture and Christian tradition present us with a type of spiritual experience that calls for our attention, an experience rooted in the sober and objective facts of redemption. We have become children of God, and we are supposed to know it.

God gives us the Holy Spirit because he wants to change our lives. He wants to help us in our prayer (Rom 8:26-27; Eph 6:18;

Jude 20b). He wants to reveal his truth to us in the scripture (1 Cor 2:10-16; 2 Cor 3:12-18). He wants to empower to serve him (Acts 1:8; 1 Cor 12:4-11). He wants to guide and direct us (Acts 13:2, 16:6-10). He wants to strengthen us so that we can live righteous and holy lives (Rom 8:3-4). Most of all, he wants us to know him personally and intimately, to enter into a relationship with him as sons and daughters (Rom 8:14-16; Gal 4:4-7). These are all purposes that he accomplishes by the gift of his Holy Spirit.

3. Life in the body of Christ. Many Christians today are awakening to the fact that God intended Christianity to be a corporate affair. Our individual lives should be situated in the context of a committed body of believers, the church. The normal Christian life is a communal life.

Most of the biblical images employed to describe the church emphasize the unity that should exist among Christians. The church is Christ's body and he is its head (Rom 12:4-5; 1 Cor 12:12-13; Eph 1:22-23, 5:23, 29-30). Therefore, "we, though many, are one body in Christ, and individually members of one another" (Rom 12:4-5). Christ and his body together constitute "one new man" (Eph 2:15). The church is a temple in which God dwells, and each individual Christian is a stone built into the structure (1 Cor 3:9, 16-17; Eph 2:19-22; 1 Pt 2:4-5). The church is God's family, his household (Eph 2:19; 1 Tm 3:14-15), and the term most commonly used in scripture to describe the Christians is "the brethren," meaning "the brothers and sisters." The church is a chosen race, a holy nation, God's own people (1 Pt 2:9). In Jesus' prayer before his passion he prays that future generations of his disciples may be united to one another as he is united to the Father, and the biblical accounts of the first church in Jerusalem focus especially on this unity of the believers (Acts 2:41-47, 4:32-35). The New Testament is thus emphatic in its testimony to the importance of living as a member of the body of Christ; it knows nothing of individualistic Christianity.

Some Christians have so spiritualized this doctrine of the church that they feel no obligation to help it become an empirical reality. According to such a view, the full unity of the church is invisible and spiritual, not to be touched or seen. However, this perspective is foreign to scripture. We do possess an invisible unity in the Holy Spirit, but this unity is supposed to be expressed and embodied in the "bond of peace" (Eph 4:3)—the cement of loving, committed relationships.

The normal Christian life involves a sharing of gifts, time, and financial resources. It involves personal support and friendship. Living the normal Christian life means identifying with the Christian people, taking a loyal stand with the Christian people locally and internationally. It also means submitting oneself to the authority of this people, acknowledging that one can no longer act as a totally independent agent. The normal Christian life is the life of a people joined to God through Jesus Christ in the Holy Spirit.

To live as part of the body of Christ should mean at least this much for all Christians. Depending upon one's confessional stance and denominational loyalty, it may imply even more— participation in sacramental life, observance of special traditions, submission to a particular teaching authority. Many of us at this conference would disagree on these matters, but we need not disagree on the basic point—active commitment to the body of Christ and immersion in its life is essential to the normal Christian life.

4. *Faithfulness to the gospel teaching.* Jesus and the apostles gave specific teaching on the Christian life that has been passed on authoritatively to us. Our task is to believe and to obey. The normal Christian life calls for nothing less.

The apostles teach us that Jesus is the Son of God, the one in whom the fullness of deity dwells. He was born of a virgin, lived a sinless life that fulfilled the law, suffered a shameful death that atoned for the sins of the human race, rose bodily from the dead, and ascended to the right hand of the Father. He will return again bodily to this world at the end of the age to gather his elect, punish the wicked, and establish a kingdom that will never end. These truths of the gospel, along with many others, form the basic kerygma that we must faithfully believe and pass on.

The apostles also pass on the words of Jesus concerning the conduct of our daily lives. They teach about those things that are forbidden to us: idolatry and witchcraft, malice and contention, adultery and fornication. The Ten Commandments are reaffirmed and underlined. In addition, we receive many positive instructions about loving personal relationships, generous financial administration, and ordered family life. These and other daily-life teachings of the gospel form the basic didache that we must faithfully receive and obey.

Our denominational position will affect how we view the basic Christian kerygma and didache. There are many important issues in the areas of sacramental theology, ecclesiology, and Mariology that divide us, as well as many differences over such practical moral issues as contraception and divorce. Nevertheless, the fundamental outlines of the basic Christian kerygma and didache are clear to all of us. They are rejected only by those who dismiss the authority of God's word in scripture.

5. Fruitfulness in life and service. The image of fruit bearing is a common one in the New Testament. It effectively communicates the principle that a right relationship with God should be manifested in the outcome of our life and work. Our character should become like that of Jesus Christ, and others should be drawn nearer to him through us.

According to the apostle Paul, the fruit of our truly living in the Holy Spirit is "love, joy, peace, patience, kindness, goodness, faithfulness, gentleness, self-control" (Gal 5:22). In other words, the normal Christian life entails a progressive transformation into the likeness of Jesus, so that we instinctively relate to people and circumstances in the way he would. The sign that we are disciples of Christ is that we walk as he walked and bear the very stamp of his character.

The normal Christian life is also a life of fruitful service. The fruit of the Holy Spirit should be expressed in good works that bring forth fruit in others' lives (Eph 2:10). In particular, evangelism and charitable work should mark the life of the Christian. The true disciple enters fully into the mission of his master, and our Master has come to reveal perfectly the love of God and to bring salvation to the world. We are called to follow after him and devote our lives to fruitful labor in his vineyard.

Fruitfulness in life and service is a basic component of the normal Christian life. Helping people to grow in the character of Christ and serve diligently in the work of his kingdom is thus an essential aspect of the goal of pastoral work.

If these five elements—commitment to Christ, life in the Holy Spirit, membership in the body, faithfulness to the gospel teaching, and fruitfulness in life and service—describe adequately the practical foundations of the normal Christian life, then they also clarify the proper goal of pastoral work. A pastoral leader's goal should be to support and encourage his flock in these basic patterns of Christian life. Each pastoral leader will also have additional goals that are distinctive and characteristic of the particular work the Lord has called him or her to. However, these additional goals should never cause us to lose sight of the pastoral imperative of summoning Christians to the normal Christian life.

The Tools of Pastoral Work

How can pastoral leaders today help people live the normal Christian life? What pastoral methods or tools will be most useful in strengthening, defending, and renewing the Christian people of the Western world in these autumn years of the twentieth century?

One of those tools I am not going to treat at length, although I think it is actually very important. This is simply preaching the gospel. One of the most fundamental needs among God's people is basic conversion to Jesus Christ and being brought into the life of God. For some people this is not conversion from serious sin—from patterns that are contrary to the Ten Commandments—but conversion from a life that is not centered upon Jesus Christ; from a life that revolves around many other concerns into a life in which Jesus Christ is the one who reigns. People need to be brought into the normal Christian life through the door of conversion, through the door of repentance and faith. Often, as we are thinking about pastoral renewal, we presume that it is mainly a matter of rekindling life that was there before. But often it is a matter of taking people whose life has never been based fully on the gospel and bringing them into a new orientation of life. Until people move into a life centered upon Christ, we can teach them as much as we want and try to get various things to happen for them, but we will find ourselves knocking on a brick wall. As soon as we really bring people to that relationship with Christ, in which he is at the heart of their lives, integrating everything else, suddenly they become docile, teachable, receptive. They are ready to change, ready to take on new patterns of life. One of the main keys to their conversion is the preaching of Jesus Christ and of what it really means to know him.

In addition to this, I believe that in our present social and cultural context there are three pastoral tools that are especially effective at helping people live lives worthy of the gospel: one-to-one discipleship, group-building, and practical teaching. These tools have proven their worth over the years among many Christians of the past and present, and I have seen their value in my own community.

One-to-one discipleship. This tool is not particularly new; Jesus employed it with the Twelve and Paul used it with Timothy. Nonetheless, pastoral leaders have often failed to realize its full potential. Robert Coleman made the point well in his book *The Master Plan of Evangelism,* and the Navigators have built much of their system of training and evangelism on this important insight. We have much to learn from their example.

We can understand this tool best by looking at each of the two terms separately. First, it is *one-to-one.* It requires that a pastoral leader make a substantial personal investment in the life of another individual. Many of the functions traditionally performed by pastoral leaders have been more directed to a large group—preaching, teaching, presiding at worship and other ceremonial occasions. These elements are all central to pastoral work, but if a pastoral leader is to help people live the normal Christian life he must also become personally involved in their individual lives.

Secondly, this tool involves *discipleship.* It is a relationship that includes teaching, training, and correction. Unlike the traditional Roman Catholic process of spiritual direction, discipleship involves more than just growth in spiritual life: it involves character formation and instruction in basic principles of Christian living and Christian service. And unlike the penitent-confessor relationship or the counselor-client relationship, a discipleship relationship is not mainly problem oriented. It focuses instead on helping a person grow into the normal Christian life. It is also not based primarily on the initiative of the individual being discipled. Instead, the pastoral leader takes the main initiative, as a teacher, to chart the course that the relationship will take.

Group-building. A second tool that is critical for the strengthening and renewing of the Christian people today is group-building. It is not enough to merely engage in one-to-one discipleship; we also need to work with individuals together to develop social environments that will strengthen them in their Christian lives and make their service more fruitful.

I have two things in mind here. The first type of groups that need to be built are groups for discipleship and accountability. In this type of group four to ten people gather regularly for the sake of sharing their lives as Christians, building one another up in the Lord, confessing weaknesses and sins, receiving encouragement and correction, and perhaps receiving teaching from a pastoral leader. Such groups played a very important role in the early Wesleyan movement (as described well by Howard Synder in his recent book, *The Radical Wesley*). They have also been very important in the Cursillo movement and in many Christian communities around the world.

The second type of group-building that pastoral leaders need to build is communal structures and environments. In times past it was customary for most pastoral leaders to presume the existence of a solid communal order, flawed by sin but still meeting many basic human needs. We live in a time of social dissolution. As Peter Williamson pointed out earlier, today this assumption is no longer realistic. Christian pastoral leaders thus have a new task in the modern setting. They must strengthen the few communal structures that still remain intact, and they must build anew wherever possible. This means above all strengthening family life—but not only the nuclear family. The nuclear family can only survive and flourish if it is set in the context of a broader network of relationships of commitment, loyalty, and trust. Where possible, we can try to strengthen the extended family, as well as attempt to rebuild stable neighborhood life. If the Christian people are to be a source of strength and life in the midst of a decaying social order, a significant pastoral investment must be made in building and supporting communal structures.

In our community we have been experimenting with combining these two types of groups: we have been building neighborhood groupings (which we call "clusters") around preexisting discipleship and accountability groups. At this point the experiment seems to be succeeding. We will know more about the potential of this approach five to ten years from now.

In passing, I will mention a third type of grouping that we need to build, one which is unfamiliar to many Christian leaders—corporate leadership groupings. These are simply groups in which pastoral leaders work together as leaders. The model has long been one of individual pastors working in their own settings. But our experience in our community and the experience of many other groups around the world has been that when you get a group of leaders really working together, it effects a revolution in the way they are able to serve. Only yesterday I was talking to a Catholic priest who is beginning to enter into a leadership role within a community. He told me what a radical difference it made to enter into a corporate ministry alongside other leaders.

Practical teaching. This is the third tool. Most pastoral leaders understand that they need to teach, but often they stop with the teaching of basic doctrine and morals. At the same time, however, their people are receiving extensive teaching through the media on sex, marriage, child rearing, emotions, finances, and the like. People are then left to sort out on their own the silver from the dross.

If we want to people to live the normal Christian life, we ought to develop and present a body of practical wisdom on living as a Christian in the modern world. If we want people to pray, then we must teach them to pray. If we want people to be more receptive to the working of the Holy Spirit, then we should teach them how they can do this. I have rarely seen Christians more frustrated than when a high ideal of Christian life is laid before them but they are not told how to live it out. A pastoral leader needs to be able to communicate practical wisdom as well as inspiration and doctrinal truth.

Practical teaching can occur in many different settings. It can be passed on to a large group, either piecemeal or in systematic form. It can be conveyed within a one-to-one discipleship relationship. It can be given in small discipleship and account-ability groups. Usually it should be done in all of these settings. The precise setting is not so important; the important thing is that it happen *somewhere*.

One-to-one discipleship, group-building, and practical teaching are three powerful tools that can be used by a pastoral leader to strengthen people in living the normal Christian life. As with any powerful tool, they can be used well or badly. Their employment does not produce a guaranteed result. However, these tools have tremendous potential for serving in the renewal of the Christian people.

Levels of Pastoral Action

The tools of pastoral work can be applied to people who are at various stages and levels of involvement with a Christian group, and they should be applied differently depending on the particular level or stage. We will look briefly at five different levels to better understand the process of application.

1. Current leaders. Christian pastoral leaders can only lead people into living the normal Christian if they are truly living that life themselves. Unfortunately, the lives of many pastoral leaders fall far short of the mark. The reasons are not difficult to find: many leaders have themselves never been trained by another leader, they have never themselves received practical teaching on how to live the normal Christian life in today's world, they have no group of peers who can provide support and accountability, and they have no broader communal support structure for their families.

The action that can be taken is simple, though not easy. First, the pastoral leader can seek out another pastoral leader of greater maturity, wisdom, experience, and stature to provide some measure of discipling in personal life and service. Secondly, he can look for a body of wisdom on how to live as a Christian and on how to serve as a Christian pastoral leader. Thirdly, he can seek relationships with other pastoral leaders of corresponding age and stature, whenever possible, who would be willing to join with him in some type of support and accountability group. The desired end is clear: pastoral leaders who are living the normal Christian life themselves and so can say confidently with the apostle Paul, "Imitate me."

2. Future pastoral leaders. Adoption of the set of approaches I am suggesting has a practical implication: we need a larger number of pastoral workers than would ordinarily operate in a church or fellowship. One or two professional pastors could not possibly disciple a body of three-hundred, five-hundred, one-thousand, or ten-thousand. The answer is not to hire an army of professional pastors but to raise up leaders from within the body who can serve as undershepherds in the care of the Christian people. This is not the same as recruiting people to serve on committees and oversee various administrative functions. Instead, it means training leaders who will actually assume significant *pastoral* responsibilities in caring for members of the body. The method of training these undershepherds should, of course, utilize all three of the tools that we have already discussed.

This model of local leadership development cannot operate

on a volunteer basis. In this system, an individual in a congregation or fellowship cannot simply choose to be a leader. Only certain people have the qualities that will enable them to fulfill this responsibility. They must be individuals of dedication and commitment, both to the Lord and to the body in which the Lord has placed them. They must have the type of strength and solidity of character that will make them a good example to others, help them to endure the special trials and difficulties that their role entails, and prevent them from becoming overly subject to what others think or feel about them. They must be capable of winning others' respect and trust. They need to be able to function as part of a team, and not simply on their own. They must be teachable and eager to be trained, free from arrogance and an overconfident investment in their own opinions and judgments.

3. Other members of the Christian body. The pastoral model which I am advocating is not geared only to a spiritual elite. It is especially effective at raising up and equipping future leaders, but it can also reach large numbers of other men and women. This is part of the burden of Coleman's work on evangelism: the one-to-one discipleship method reaches fewer people in the short-run than a mass rally, but in the long-run it is more effective in quality and quantity as each "generation" of disciples raises up another. The Wesleyan movement amply demonstrates the numerical potential of discipleship and accountability groups. This pastoral model can have a considerable impact on a large number of people.

Group-building and practical teaching are especially important in caring for the body as a whole. If we construct the proper communal environments and found them solidly on the foundation of Christ and his truth, then individuals will not need an intensive regimen of continual pastoral oversight. This is all the more the case if the members of the body receive the proper instruction and formation as they enter the body. This brings us to our next level of concern.

4. New members. For those who are just becoming Christians and entering the life of God's people, the basic pastoral tools need to be used in a another distinctive pastoral configuration. Those entering a body of people who are really living the normal Christian life need a period of transition in which old patterns of life are left behind and new patterns are adopted. The change required is too significant to occur in an instant, though a fundamental shift in orientation of life may only take that long. A new member of the body needs a period of time that can act as a kind of decompression chamber, or, to use another water image, as a lock in a canal system. The more the Christian people live a way of life distinct from the world around them, the more it will be necessary to provide an effective transition period for those entering this life.

The one-to-one discipleship during this period will concentrate especially on winning faith and confidence in the Lord Jesus and commitment to his people. A discipleship group for such people will be geared mainly to giving them a smooth time of transition, welcoming them warmly to a new way of life without diluting the fullness of the gospel call. Such a group would largely consist of people in the same transitional position in the body and would be led by a mature and experienced Christian man or woman. New members can also be gradually introduced to the network of communal family relationships that serve as an infrastructure for the life of the body. The practical teaching during this period focuses on the most basic elements of the Christian life, such as repentance, faith, love of God and love of neighbor, prayer, and Bible study.

People being evangelized. Evangelism is a central element in the normal Christian life. The Great Commission gives us one main reason why the church exists—it is an ark of salvation that is supposed to continually gather new passengers. The church is on a rescue mission within the world. Evangelism also strengthens the church, injecting new gifts and resources into its bloodstream.

Like pastoral care, evangelism can only go so far on programmatic activities. Such activities make an important contribution in both the pastoral and the evangelistic spheres, but they are inadequate by themselves. Some type of one-to-one evangelism is as important as some type of one-to-one discipleship. It is usually through contact with another individual—friend, relative, coworker, or neighbor—that a person breaks through into the realm of faith in Christ. The importance of a personal one-to-one investment should not be minimized.

It is also helpful to introduce an interested aquaintance to a Christian environment that can attract him or her to the Lord. Christian group-building will here provide us with such environments of loving relationships. In addition, those sharing in a common accountability grouping can support one another in their evangelistic efforts (this was an especially crucial element in the Cursillo approach to small groups).

The main way that practical teaching can serve the work of evangelism is by equipping members of the body with the salty wisdom that makes preaching the gospel so much easier. As in most areas of the Christian life, there are an almost infinite number of mistakes that we can (and do) make in evangelism, and practical instruction from someone experienced and gifted in fishing for men and women can prevent much grief.

The approaches to pastoral care that I am proposing are based on the conviction that the normal Christian life is a high and challenging call, but that it is also attainable by large numbers of normal Christians. Our experience in The Word of God, the community of which I am a member, confirms this conviction. Quality and quantity need not be at odds with one another. They can be reconciled, though only with great patience.

There is one particular element of the normal Christian life that this pastoral approach seeks to especially cultivate, and on which it depends for its success: commitment and dedication. A group of Christians can progress a long way even with little wisdom if they have the right level of commitment to the Lord and commitment to one another. The importance of this quality and the means of fostering it have been discussed by Douglas Hyde in his book *Dedication and Leadership*. As he astutely observes, in this century the Marxists have often done better at producing dedicated disciples than have the Christians. If we are to be the light of the world and the salt of the earth, then we must be wholeheartedly committed to the cause of Christ. Otherwise our light will burn only dimly and our salt will lose its savor.

It may not be immediately obvious how to apply all these principles to the various pastoral settings that exist among the Christian churches. My intention here has only been to suggest a reorientation in our pastoral mentality that can open us up to exploring new methods and strategies which may increase our effectiveness in confronting the enormous challenges of the modern world and the modern church. These pastoral principles would apply differently to different types of Christian settings. They can be applied most completely by pastors working in fellowships, congregations, and parishes that have the potential of becoming fully renewed Christian communities. Such communities can serve as models of pastoral renewal and as sources of wisdom and encouragement. In other bodies a pastoral leader may be unable to apply these principles to the whole congregation but could work with a smaller subgrouping within the body, while using a more conventional pastoral model for the wider congregation, at least for a certain period of time. These pastoral principles can also apply in various ways to other Christian institutions such as schools, seminaries, celibate communities, missionary bodies, and Christian businesses. Finally, it would be possible to establish wider movements which embody these pastoral perspectives and which touch the lives of large numbers of people. Examples of this would be a Christian family movement, a movement of pastors organized together for fraternal care or correction, and a popular evangelistic and discipleship movement.

In whatever setting we are working, however, the goal of all our efforts should be the same: that the people of God might live a life worthy of the gospel of Christ and witness fittingly to his saving grace. Above all, the work of renewal demands the gracious intervention of God. Ingenious human techniques and sweaty human efforts can never substitute for the vitality and power that come from above. "Unless the Lord builds the house, those who build it labor in vain" (Ps 127:1). The normal Christian life is lived by faith and by the power of the Holy Spirit, and normal Christian pastoral work must operate according to the same principle. Ultimately, the most important element in any quest for renewal is imitation of the fervent prayer of the psalmist, "Restore us, O God; let thy face shine, that we may be saved!" (Ps 80:3, 7, 19).

Notes

Introduction
Christianity Confronts Modernity

1. Joseph Bayly, "The How-To Church," *Eternity,* Jan. 1983, p. 14.
2. Edward Shorter, *The Making of the Modern Family* (New York: Basic Books, 1977), p. 278.
3. Peter Laslett, *The World We Have Lost* (New York: Charles Scribner's Sons, 1965), p. 45.
4. Michael Anderson, *Family Structure in Nineteenth Century Lancashire* (London: Cambridge University Press, 1971), p. 82.
5. Peter Laslett, *op. cit.,* p. 9.
6. Marion J. Levy, Jr., *Modernization: Latecomers and Survivors* (New York: Basic Books, 1972), p. 5.
7. Christopher Dawson, *The Judgment of the Nations* (New York: Sheed and Ward, 1942), pp. 103-4.
8. Os Guinness, "The Subversive Society," *Pastoral Renewal,* Feb. 1983, p. 55.
9. James Hitchcock, "The Secular City, 1981," *The National Catholic Register,* p. 1.
10. Peter Berger, "Secular Theology and the Rejection of the Supernatural: Reflections on Recent Trends," *Theological Studies* 38, 1977, pp. 39-56.
11. George W. Dollar, *A History of Fundamentalism in America* (Greenville, S.C.: Bob Jones University Press, 1973), p. 177.
12. Donald Bloesch, "The Challenge Facing the Churches," Peter Williamson and Kevin Perrotta, eds., *Christianity Confronts Modernity* Ann Arbor, Mich.: Servant, 1981), pp. 215, 218.
13. Cited by Alexander Tomsky, " 'Pacem in Terris' between Church and State in Czechoslovakia," *Religion in Communist Lands* 10, 1982, p. 279.

Chapter One
Self, Jesus, and God: The Roots of Religious Secularization

1. James Hitchcock, "The Course of Radical Change in the Churches," *Christianity Confronts Modernity,* Peter Williamson and Kevin Perrotta, eds. (Ann Arbor, Mich.: Servant Publications, 1981), pp. 91-110.

147

Chapter Three
The Attack on God's Word—And the Response

1. R. Scroggs, "Tradition, Freedom and the Abyss," *New Theology*, no. 8., ed. Martin E. Marty and Dean G. Peerman (New York: Macmillan, 1971), pp. 85, 100.
2. "Readers Forum," *The Catholic Messenger* (Davenport, Iowa), Sept. 13, 1979, p. 8.
3. St. Hippolytus of Rome, "Fragment" in Eusebius, *History of the Church*, 5, ch. 28.
4. R. Barr, Editorial, *Today's Parish*, Jan. 1980, p. 5ff.
5. St. Augustine, *On Christian Doctrine*, II, VII, 9 (38-9).
6. Quoted by Rev. Msgr. J.T. Ellis, "American Catholics in 1979," *The Pilot* (Boston, Mass.), Sept. 21, 1979, p. 9.
7. R.H. Springer, S.J., "Holy God, Gays Want In!" *Today's Parish*, Jan. 1980, pp. 10-13.
8. Dr. Deane Ferm, "'The Road Ahead in Theology' Revisited," *The Christian Century*, May 9, 1979, pp. 524-27.

Chapter Four
The Loss of a Christian Way of Life

1. "Belief and the Bible: A Crisis of Authority?" *Christianity Today*, March 21, 1980, pp. 20-23.
2. Quoted by Charles A. Savitskas, "Portrait: The American Catholic Family," *Our Sunday Visitor Magazine*, Dec. 12, 1982, p. 7.
3. Quoted by Robert Lockwood, "Comparison: The 1950s' Catholic Family and Today's," *Our Sunday Visitor Magazine*, Nov. 28, 1982, p. 6.
4. "Forty-one Percent of Adults in U.S. Attended Church in Typical Week of '82," *Emerging Trends*, Jan. 1983, p. 1; "Sunday Activities in Canada," *Emerging Trends*, Sept. 1982, p. 5; Princeton Religion Research Center, *Religion in America 1979-1980* (Princeton, N.J.: PRRC, undated), p. 37; "Remarkable Stability Noted in Basic Trends in Religion," *Emerging Trends*, Feb. 1982, p. 1.
5. George Banner, "Surprising Facts about Christian Consumers," *Christian Advertising Forum*, June-July 1982.
6. "Christians Divorcing—Symptom of a Weakened Church," *Pastoral Renewal*, Mar. 1980, p. 75.
7. Steve Clapp, *Teenage Sexuality: A Crisis and an Opportunity for the Church* (Sidell, Ill.: C-4 Resources, 1981), pp. 3-4, 18.
8. "A Profile of the American Catholic Family," *America*, Sept. 27, 1980.
9. *The Gallup Youth Survey*, Dec. 16, 1981.
10. Edward Shorter, *The Making of the Modern Family* (New York: Basic Books, 1975), p. 108.

11. *Connecticut Mutual Life Report on American Values in the '80s: The Impact of Belief* (Hartford, Conn.: Connecticut Mutual Life).
12. Kenneth Kantzer, "Reflections: Five Years of Change," *Christianity Today*, Nov. 26, 1982.

Chapter Five
*Orthodox, Protestants, Roman Catholics:
What Basis for Cooperation?*

1. Anita and Peter Deyneka, Jr., "A Salvation of Suffering," *Christianity Today*, July 16, 1982, p. 20.
2. Peter Berger, "Secular Theology and the Rejection of the Supernatural: Reflections on Recent Trends," *Theological Studies* 38, 1977, pp. 39-56.
3. Christopher Dawson, *op. cit.*, p. 160.
4. *Ibid.*, p. 171.
5. *Ibid.*, p. 178.
6. *Ibid.*, p. 179.

Chapter Six
Steps to the Renewal of the Christian People

1. Quoted from T.H.L. Parker, *The Oracles of God: An Introduction to the Preaching of John Calvin* (London: Lutterworth Press, 1947), p. 60.
2. Note especially the pioneer studies by J. Edwin Orr of post-Methodist awakenings: *The Second Evangelical Awakening in Britain* (London: Marshall, Morgan & Scott, 1949); *The Second Evangelical Awakening in America* (Grand Rapids, Mich.: Zondervan, 1952); *The Fervent Prayer: The World Wide Impact of the Great Awakening of 1858* (Chicago: Moody Press, 1974) (all three dealing with the movement of 1957-60); *The Eager Feet: Evangelical Awakenings, 1790-1830* (Chicago: Moody Press, 1975); *The Flaming Tongue: Evangelical Awakenings, 1900-1910* (Chicago: Moody Press, 2nd ed., 1975); *The Light of the Nations: Evangelical Renewal and Advance in the Nineteenth Century* (Exeter: Paternoster Press and Grand Rapids: Eerdmans, 1965); *Campus Aflame: Evangelical Awakenings in College Communities* (Glendale, Calif.: Regal Books, 1971); *Evangelical Awakenings in Southern Asia* (Glendale, Calif.: Regal Books, 1971); *Evangelical Awakenings in Southern Asia* (Minneapolis, Minn.: Bethany Fellowship, 1975); *Evangelical Awakenings in Africa* (Minneapolis: Bethany Fellowship, 1975); *Evangelical Awakenings in the South Seas* (Minneapolis: Bethany Fellowship, 1976). Note also J.T. Carson, *God's River in Spate* (Presbyterian Church of Ireland, 1958; on the Irish revival of 1859); J. Goforth, *By My Spirit* (Grand Rapids, Mich.: Zondervan, 1967; on the Chinese revivals of 1908); E. Eifion Evans, *When He*

Is Come (Bridgend, Wales: Evangelical Press of Wales; 2nd ed., 1967; on the Welsh revival of 1859); and *The Welsh Revival of 1904* (Bridgend, Wales: Evangelical Press of Wales, 1969).
3. Richard F. Lovelace, *Dynamics of Spiritual Life* (Downer's Grove, Ill.: InterVarsity Press, 1979), pp. 21f.
4. *Op.cit.*, especially chapter 2.
5. Arthur Wallis, *In the Day of Thy Power* (London: Christian Literature Crusade, 1956), p. 20.
6. Duncan Campbell, *The Lewis Awakening 1949-1953* (Edinburgh: Faith Mission, 1954), p. 29.
7. John Howe, *Works* (London: F. Westley and A.H. Davis, 1832), p. 575.
8. Charles G. Finney, *Revivals of Religion* (London: Oliphants, 1928), p. 20.

An Agenda for Theology

James I. Packer

THEOLOGY IS A COMPLEX of disciplines—exegesis, biblical theology, historical theology, systematics, symbolics, ethics, apologetics, liturgics, missiology, spirituality, pastoral theology, and more—but in essence it is one threefold activity throughout: listening to God's utterances in scripture, testifying to what one has heard, and testing all human utterances and behavior, past and present, in and outside the church, by what the Bible says. Theology is meant to function in the church as both disinfectant and nutrient, sterilizing and fertilizing our minds, guiding our wills and desires, stirring our imaginations, calling forth our praises, informing our pastoral care, and focusing our message to the world. Theology thus has a vital contribution to make to the church's life.

Because theology's task is to reinterpret the unchanging gospel in such a way that every generation may understand its substance and perceive its relevance, the church's theologians must have their mental windows open not only to the warm rays of Christian tradition but also to the cold blasts of secular thought. Yet in their listening and responding to the world they must not let go their Christian identity nor forget their churchly function. A theologian who gets swamped by the secularity with which he interacts is someone whom the church can do without. "The place for the ship is in the sea," said D.L. Moody, speaking of the church in the world, "but God help the ship if the sea gets into it." Sadly, however, much academic theology has in recent years gotten swamped and waterlogged in this way, and large segments of the church have been weakened as a result.

To understand this situation, one must take account not only of the resurgence of that post-Enlightenment relativism and skepticism which by the turn of this century had spawned both Protestant liberalism and Catholic modernism, but also of the sociology of the presentday theologian's trade. To achieve a career as a theological academic one has to find employment in a teaching or research institution, and to do that one has to impress potential employers as being likely to make a significant contribution in one's own field, and to do that one has to have a point of view of which they can approve. If one viewpoint comes to dominate the minds of those who manage academic institutions, it immediately becomes harder for scholars who do not share that point of view to get jobs. This fact soon creates the optical illusion that most significant scholars are on the one side! Again, an academic who has got his feet on the ladder and wants to climb professionally (and there is nothing wrong with such a purpose) must publish in approved journals and with approved publishers, be seen and if possible heard at conferences of learned societies, and join in the ongoing debates among his peers. In such circumstances it is the easiest thing in the world to forget one's churchly identity and responsibilities and simply think along with generally accepted opinion, concerning oneself only with keeping in the swim. In this, of course, theology does not differ from any other academic field, and I do not mention these things in order to censure them. I mention them only to explain how it was possible for the current landslide into theological relativism among Catholics, and the parallel landslides among Protestants into such things as Bultmannism and situation ethics, to take place.

In academic theology today we face an extraordinary diversity of specific opinions held together by an equally extraordinary consensus as to what academically worthwhile opinions will be like. Most of the time it is simply taken for granted that any views which merit academic consideration will be tentative and concessive, opposed to the categories of heresy and blasphemy as being invalid, tolerant of pluralism as being stimulating, intolerant of orthodoxies as being hostile to intellectual enterprise, and observably different in some way from the received wisdom. Novelty is at a premium, as once it was at Athens, and reassertions of traditional views evoke little enthusiasm within our theological establishments. The restless, skeptical spirit of our age has deeply infected the theological world, and the result is that in many Christian minds the outlines of historic Christian faith have crumbled, and the content of that faith has been obscured, in just the same way as the features of weathering statues grow increasingly indistinct, to the point where they are quite unrecognizable. In this bleak milieu all significant theological study and debate takes place today, for this is the mainstream. There are backwaters, to be sure, where theologians of particular conservative traditions meet together, but such meetings make little difference to what goes on in the mainstream. And out in that stream there are few points of classical Christian theology which have not become matters of struggle and dispute.

Thus, there is struggle over *the Bible.* Should we trust its history? How far may we pick and choose among its varied theological contents? Should we give up the idea of biblical teaching as revealed truth in favor of a theology of story, or of existential encounter with God through the evocative impact of Bible words? How, from what scripture meant historically, should we determine what it means for us? How, in the light of its doctrine, should we make ethical decisions? And so on.

Then there is a struggle over the doctrine of *God* and of *Jesus Christ.* Is God finite? evolving? impassible? Is he intrinsically and eternally triune, or does the doctrine of the Trinity just express three aspects of our experience of God who in himself is unipersonal? Can one distinguish God as he is in himself from God in relation to his creatures? Is there validity in the doctrine of the Incarnation, which states that the eternal Son took humanness without his deity being diminished, or should we see this as myth and the Jesus of history as just a particularly godly man? When and how should God the Father and Jesus the Son be recognized in non-Christian religions (for it is nowadays axiomatic that they should be)? Et cetera, et cetera.

Also there is struggle over the doctrine of *salvation*. Is the Anselmic, transactional ideas of the atonement, according to which the Son offered himself in death to the Father as a satisfaction for sin, believable? Should not all atonement language be interpreted subjectively, of the Christian's changed relationship to God, rather than objectively, of the divine act that was the basis of that change? How should believers view the cross of Christ? Should not universal salvation through the cross be asserted? Is it conceivable that anyone can be eternally lost, and that hell will have permanent residents? Are not all mankind in a state of grace by virtue of the cross? Is it a matter of priority in our service of others to lead them, if we can, to conversion, or are other forms of service more important? The debates continue.

It has long been taken for granted that the deepest theological differences, at least in the West, are those dividing Protestants from Roman Catholics. The assumption is that all Protestants are closer to each other in thought than any of them are to Roman Catholics, and vice versa. Perhaps it once was so, but the sample questions just cited make us aware that it is not so today. They are all quite fundamental to one's view of Christianity, and they are agitated with equal vehemence on both sides of the Reformation divide. The truth is that the deepest contemporary cleavage in theology is between those who may be labelled traditionalists and radicals respectively—"trads" and "rads"; that is, between those for whom the God-givenness of all biblical teaching, and of the historic faith as therein set forth, are fixed points, and those for whom they are not. This division cuts across the Roman Catholic Church, just as it does across all the older Protestant church families. On the one side are those who still affirm the ontological Trinity, the divine sovereignty, the incarnation of the Son of God, the transactional atonement, faith in Jesus as the way of eternal life, the divine-human mediator as the focus of devotion, the primacy of evangelism in mission, the absoluteness of biblical moral teaching, and the need of orthodoxy as a basis for right living (orthopraxy). On the other side are those who think that they may and must treat all these historic affirmations as culturally conditioned symbols, open to any form of reinterpretation which strikes the theologian as meaningful for today. It is obvious that these attitudes reflect different and incompatible views of the nature of the divine realities to which theological statements made in the church refer, and this is a more fundamental division than that over any particular doctrine.

It is a recognized principle of Christian ecumenism, and also of common sense, that we should not do separately what we can better do together. It seems clear from what has been said that maintaining the basic ingredients of the historic faith against their opponents in and outside the church is something that can better be done by Catholics and Protestants working together than by either battalion of "trads" working separately. So I conclude that our times call for an overt alliance of conservative theologians from both stables, an axis relationship finding expression in a joint academic strategy, whereby more effective breakwaters against the erosive and distorting effect of the pounding waves of modernity in Christian minds may be set up.

Such an alignment would helpfully clarify what is actually going on in our churches. It would strengthen the hands of those who at an academic level are currently laboring to keep open the old paths, and finding themselves isolated as they do so. It would give layfolk resources for assessing what their official theological leaders say. And its long-term ecumenical and pastoral potential is beyond our power to calculate. For Protestant and Catholic theological conservatives thus to cooperate, in these areas where they are in fact fundamentally agreed, would certainly enrich both sides (no one who has had experience of joint Protestant-Catholic theological work will doubt that), and should equally certainly further the cause of God and truth in all our churches. New associational structures and conference patterns will be called for, but these should not be hard to mount, given the vision and the will. The project is surely a practical one.

This is a venture that we badly need. Shall I see it made in my lifetime? God knows—but I hope so.

An Agenda for Christian Ethics

Germain Grisez

CHRISTIAN ETHICS ought to be centered on our Lord Jesus. To be Christocentric means that Christian ethics should guide followers of Jesus toward more perfect personal union with him. This union primarily is a sharing by the grace of the Spirit in Jesus' divine life. But it also is a human communion in bodily life and in cooperative work. Ethics bears directly upon the last.

Christians are called to do what Jesus did and add to it, to bear real and abundant fruit, not by themselves but in him. Without Jesus we can do nothing; in him we can and ought to do great things. Thus, Christian ethics should be an ethics of communal cooperation with Jesus; each Christian should seek and accept his or her personal role and responsibilities in the body of Christ.

The work of Jesus bears on human salvation, begun in this world but completed only in heavenly fulfillment. Hence, Christian ethics primarily should be an other-worldly humanism. It should direct Christian life here and now as a real sharing in the kingdom (which is not of this world) and preparation for everlasting life (still to come).

A truly Christocentric ethics must be a Trinitarian ethics. Human persons are made in God's image, and their fulfillment can only be in renewal according to the loving plan God proposed from the beginning. The focus of Christian ethics on the kingdom must not mean a religious fanaticism or even an exclusive focus on the good of religion. All human goods are affected by sin, redeemed by God in Jesus, and ought to be reverenced and served by Christians.

Nor can a genuinely Christocentric ethics be individualistic;

God calls us to heavenly fellowship, not simply to saving my soul and your soul. The ethics of Jesus is that of the New Covenant. Turning from sin, Christians make a fundamental option or decision for Jesus, accept with faith the terms of the covenant sealed with his blood, rely with confident hope on God's faithfulness to his promises, and fulfill their communal responsibilities by the love which is the gift of the Holy Spirit.

Moreover, just as Jesus' divinity was no substitute for his living his human life, and his human life accomplished nothing without the power of the Spirit, so grace is no substitute for Christians' fulfilling their human responsibilities, yet human works are fruitless except through the power of the Spirit. A truly Christian ethics does not use God's grace as an excuse for sloth.

Christian ethics ought to be rooted in the word of God.

For Christian ethics to be rooted in God's word, that word must be heard and accepted in faith from those who hand it on. A genuinely Christian ethics will be faithful to God's revealed word as it is received in the community of faith and will resist every attempt to substitute supposed inner movements of the Spirit for faithful obedience to the truth of the gospel.

One can think out the problems of Christian ethics only if one is a believer striving to live a Christian life. Theological work requires scholarship, but a Christian scholar must not allow the world to define what is scholarly (what agrees with the academic establishment's methods and opinions) and what is not (what is faithful to the word of God which the nonbelieving academic world rejects). Authentic Christian scholarship is marked by absolute obedience to God's word, even when one does not understand it and finds oneself at a loss for plausible answers to the challenges of nonbelievers.

The fundamental mysteries of faith—Trinity; Incarnation, and second birth of men and women by the gift of the Spirit— must be seen as practical truths which should shape human life. The Bible also includes specific, revealed moral truths whose validity is absolute and unalterable. These include the Ten Commandments.

However, Christian ethics cannot be limited to the norms explicitly stated in the Bible. The principles explicitly contained in scripture—especially those exemplified by Jesus' living of his own human life—are endlessly rich in consequences for every question of life in every time and place.

The Bible must be interpreted as a living word. Christians of diverse denominations obviously differ about how to do this. This difference is not insignificant, but all agree on the primacy of the word and the need to understand it within the community of faith. Christian ethics should be ecumenical; it should work toward cooperation among those who accept Jesus as Lord in faithfully unfolding the meaning of God's word for today.

The relationship between law and grace must not be misunderstood. Love fulfills the law and renders it unnecessary as law—that is, as something imposed upon a sinful and resistant, fallen humankind. But love does not nullify or displace the truth about human good and evil. The grace of the Holy Spirit, won for us by Christ, instead renews human hearts and enables men and women, living in Christ, to walk in the full light of the moral truth which God has made clear to humankind in Jesus.

Christian ethics ought to make use of a rationally defensible ethical theory.

Reliance on the word of God does not mean that Christian ethics can be an intuitionism which neglects or bypasses careful study of facts and reasoned application of principles to problems. The word of God comes in human words, and the Spirit normally speaks to us through careful study, critical reflection, and charitable dialogue with one another.

Christians often have been suspicious of philosophy, and rightly so if it tries to usurp the role of faith. But philosophy need not be dogmatic; it need not try to produce an autonomous rational worldview. It can limit itself modestly to a responsible

use of reason articulating and defending that part of the truth of
the Christian faith which is accessible to reason, clarifying the
meaning of linguistic and other symbols in which (and against
which) faith must be articulated and applied, and pointing to
human realities, present in our awareness, which faith illumi-
nates and renews.

A Christian philosophy of this sort is needed for four reasons.
First, the Christian must be ready to give an account, and
cannot do this without such a reasoned view. Second, the
Christian must understand the reality of the world and be able
to criticize the inadequate theories nonbelievers offer to make
sense of and guide life. Third, the believer must be able to draw
out new implications of the word of God to meet new challenges
and cannot do this without a systematic theory of morality.
Fourth, one cannot interpret scripture without a unified
worldview—that is, a philosophy. Failure to develop a consciously Christian philosophy leads to the unconscious use of
some non-Christian philosophy.

There are several urgent challenges today for the theoretical
part of Christian ethics. A sound account of conscience is
needed to counter the subjectivist notion that individuals may
folow their autonomous opinions against moral truth, even that
which is clearly included in God's word. The subjective and
objective aspects of morality must be carefully distinguished,
and the objective truth of moral norms clarified. The right way
of reaching moral judgments must be explained and the error
shown in reducing morality to efficiency in attaining specific
objectives.

Christian ethics ought to be truly pastoral.

Christian ethics must be realistic about sin and the truth of
the human condition. The first principle of pastoral practice is
honesty about the fallen human condition. The first pastoral act
is the call for repentance. God's mercy demands conversion and
enables fallen men and women to rise to a new life.

Christian ethics should effectively guide preaching, teaching, and counseling. To do this, it must take into account the actual challenges and temptations people face today. But with this realism, it should articulate the way of the Lord Jesus as really livable, not merely by an elite but by all. A truly pastoral approach not only asks and answers the question, "What must I do?" but the further questions, "How am I to do it? What can I do right now?"

To ask and answer these questions, the Christian ethicist must be confident in the power of the Spirit. This confidence does not exclude but rather requires full use of human means, including sound psychological insights and techniques, for building up a Christian character. Realism also demands the building up of Christian community. Christian ethics should not be individualistic; it must always stress mutual help, the bearing of one another's burdens.

Mature life in Christ requires not only initial conversion but continuing conversion. Each Christian must learn how to put Jesus in the center of his or her life and subject everything else in life to his lordship. This means setting priorities for one's whole life, determining the use of one's lifetime, finding one's personal vocation.

In its pastoral function, a Christian ethics must clarify the role and right use of discernment. This is necessary to determine one's personal vocation and to exclude from one's life those concerns which, though not morally objectionable in themselves, have no place in God's plan. In Christian discernment, advice and guidance of the community is necessary, because God's will for each Christian is expressed through the institutional forms of the ecclesial body.

A truly pastoral theology is not legalistic; it does not regard the requirements of Christian life as a set of arbitrary rules which can be bent and stretched to lighten the burden of following Jesus. Thus, Christian ethics should firmly reject dissent from the word of God. A truly pastoral Christian ethics will help leaders of the community know how to deal effectively with such dissent by making clear that false teaching lacks authority while authentic teaching shares in the authority of

God's word, which it guards as sacred and faithfully proposes.

Confidence in the Spirit also means firm rejection of any "theory of compromise"—that is, that in our fallen world sin is sometimes required. Similarly, the theory that a good end can justify one in destroying, damaging, or impeding human life or other goods intrinsic to human persons must be rejected both as rationally incoherent and as a betrayal of faith's teaching that certain kinds of acts, such as idolatry, adultery, and killing the innocent, are always grave evils.

An Agenda for Christians and Psychology

Paul C. Vitz

THE FOLLOWING IS A SUMMARY, inevitably somewhat personal, of a wide-ranging, two-hour meeting of over thirty participants at the conference. The purpose of the workshop was to identify those issues and problems of special relevance to Christians engaged in pastoral and counseling activities. We did not really discuss any of the topics at length; instead they were brought up or identified because they were thought important and in need of careful reflection, analysis, observation, and study. Thus, the list is, in many respects, one of potential issues for future research and writing.

In fact, many of the questions raised below have already received attention from Christian psychologists. In some instances, there exist very important Christian contributions, but no attempt was made to identify them during the discussion. At the very least, the questions show a widespread need both for a more effective method of disseminating the existing contributions of Christian psychologists, and for much more research and writing in this broad area of concern.

The points raised in the discussion concerned either general problems or issues, or specific questions or statements of need. Among the general issues were these:

1. We need a much better understanding of the distinction between the psychological and the spiritual. In particular, spiritual and religious aspects of people's lives seem to be misinterpreted as being psychological in nature. Somehow psychology has expanded far beyond its legitimate boundaries. This problem has become particularly acute in seminary training.

2. We need an integrated, positive Christian psychology of the person and a knowledge of how this theory relates to psychotherapy, with special reference to how it contrasts with secular models of the person. Such a psychology should include concepts relevant to child psychology, and the special problems of religion and abnormal psychology.

3. We need a good scriptural or biblical counseling psychology—one which identifies the psychological implications of scripture in a way that maintains an authentic understanding of the passage, but avoids oversimplified scripture quoting and makes useful psychological contact with the person needing psychological help. That is, what is needed is a solidly Christian psychological bridge from scripture to the person's problem.

4. We need a Christian psychology of homosexuality which maintains the historical Christian position, but also offers some real help for homosexuals willing to work toward change. A similar psychology is needed for heterosexuals caught in promiscuous or adulterous ways of living.

5. We need a Christian psychology of the virtues and of Christian character. For example, what is the psychology of courage? chastity? patience? honesty? humility?

6. Closely related to the preceding point is the need for a psychology of the will and of self-control. Many people today seem to be controlled primarily by their feelings. They constantly find themselves out of control and incapable of being even reasonably reliable or trustworthy in their interpersonal relationships, still less in their moods and attitudes. They are incapable of disciplining themselves or others.

7. Where can one go to get an understanding of the differences between male and female psychology? Male psychology can be baffling to many women, and vice versa.

These were some of the more specific questions which were mentioned:

1. How can you deal with people who certainly need counseling or psychological help, but who adamantly refuse it, often to the continued detriment of themselves or others?

2. In contrast, what can be done to avoid getting trapped in

a pastoral or counseling relationship with someone who constantly "needs help"? How do you avoid unproductive, time-consuming dependency relationships? How can you say no constructively?

3. How can one place in a Christian framework—and also deepen the understanding of—an inner healing experience that may have been carried out in a context of secular psychology (e.g., a Jungian framework)?

4. How does one recognize one's limits as a counselor and know when someone should be referred? A related question is, what does a pastor need to know so that he can make intelligent referrals to Christian psychologists? That is, how does one recognize a psychologist as both Christian and competent? After all, some who claim to be Christian psychologists may just be interested in money or in pushing their own peculiar interpretation of Christianity. Or they may really be secular psychologists whose faith is irrelevant to their practice.

5. Related to the preceding questions is the problem of recognizing when a psychological problem is fundamentally a biological one. For example, how might one recognize that a person's depression is really a recurring biochemical imbalance, and neither psychological nor spiritual in origin?

6. We need to know what to do with people who have already had a heavy dose of a particular secular psychology before they seek out Christian help. For example, what do you do with someone whose mind-set is already strongly determined by life scripts, est, self-actualization, etc.?

7. How can the Christian ideal, that is, the life of the serious Christian, be shown to be psychologically practical and not an impossible dream?

8. We need a Christian psychology for hard times; in particular, a psychology of suffering.

9. What are the problems and dangers for the practitioner in making the transition from a secular to a Christian psychologist?

10. Where can one be trained in Christian psychology? in secular psychology in a Christian environment?

11. We need more case histories of Christian counseling and psychotherapy, more detailed examples of such counseling in action, with many different types of problems. Also needed is a booklet series on Christian approaches to such things as depression, anger, anxiety—a kind of Christian-help psychology.

12. We need a greater visibility of Christian psychology, of Christian psychologists—and perhaps an institute or some official center or clearing house for the many complex and varied issues raised by the emergence of Christian psychology.

A Note about Membership

AT THE END of the Christianity Confronts Modernity-II conference in October 1982, most of the participants joined in an association which has taken the name . . . Alliance for Faith and Renewal and has expressed its purposes in the statement that appears at the beginning of this book.

Members have either attended one of the two Christianity Confronts Modernity conferences or have read one of the books coming from the conferences or have listened to the tapes. Agreeing to the statement of purpose, members commit themselves to study, prayer, and communication on the topics of the conferences for the good of the whole Christian people. Members work in various spheres of responsibility, but are interested in finding ways to cooperate and to offer each other brotherly and sisterly Christian support.

At present, the Alliance is sponsored by the Center for Pastoral Renewal, which organized the conferences. The Center publishes a quarterly newsletter for the Alliance, and also sends Alliance members the Center's own quarterly newsletter, called *Center Update*. The Center plans to sponsor another conference for the Alliance. As of summer 1983 the date and program of the next conference were undetermined, as the Center pursued consultation with Alliance members regarding future direction for the Alliance.

For a membership application write to the Center for Pastoral Renewal, P.O. Box 8617, Ann Arbor, Michigan 48107 U.S.A.